CLAIRE LLOYD discovered her artistic talent at an early age and hasn't stopped since; she went on to establish an international career as a designer, art director, photographer and film maker. Her influence can be seen in magazines, interiors and advertising campaigns across the world. With her exquisite eye for detail and a focus on simplicity and clean lines, she has transformed properties in London, Sydney and Greece, where she now spends most of her time. *My Greek Island Home* is her second book.

clairelloyd.com

My Greek Island Home

text and photography
Claire Lloyd

LANTERN
an imprint of
PENGUIN BOOKS

for Dad, Mum
and Matthew

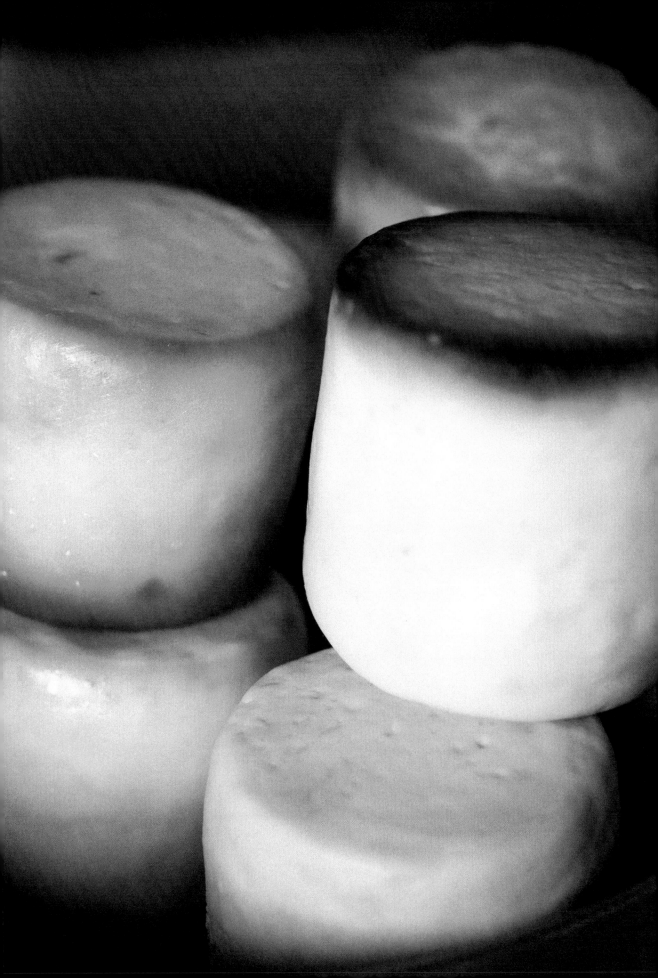

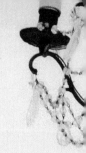

Contents

Φεύγοντας
Leaving

The world awaits! off on my
first big journey—school.

In 1983 I left Australia to live in London; I had backpacked around Europe, an experience that opened my eyes and left me longing to see more, but now I was going abroad to live. On the way to the airport, my father, through his tears, gave me the following advice: 'Don't talk to anyone you don't know.' Through my tears, I agreed, although I knew it was a promise I couldn't keep. My plan was to be gone for a year, to expand my work experience and travel through Europe again. I accomplished both; however, I never made it home.

My memories of growing up in suburban Sydney in the Sixties and Seventies are of long hot summers, Balmoral Beach, picnics in the garden, sweet-smelling magnolia, bushes laden with gardenias, the cool spray of sprinklers, fishing trips, ballet lessons, Saturday netball matches and games of cricket. Home was loving and supportive – our parents always encouraged my brother, my sister and me to live life to the full. They taught us that if you worked hard, everything was possible.

My mother is imaginative and creative, and made even the most mundane chores into a game; we were always entertained and stimulated. She would collect a car full of neighbouring children and take us all fishing. She coached netball teams and my brother's soccer team, made our clothes, ran lamington drives, organised fashion shows and did whatever it took to raise money for our schools. My father worked extremely hard six days a week, so we did not see him very much. I tease him now about how scared we were of him. It was during our annual holiday to The Entrance on the Central Coast of New South Wales that Dad came into his own. Here he would take us to the beach, and fish and play cricket with us. He also enjoyed a (fiercely competitive, it must be said) game of Monopoly.

My first job was in a very small advertising agency that specialised in retail. My mother had spotted the position in the local paper. Cunningly, she promised me new clothes if my application was successful. I got the job and started just before Christmas. My boss, John, seemed like a dinosaur at the age of twenty-nine. One of the first things he told me was, 'It's better to make a decision, even if it isn't the right one, than to make no decision at all.' I took him at his word and managed to make all kinds of decisions, good and bad.

My time there was fun and I learned a lot. Drawing was something I loved and both my mum and her mum (my nanna) encouraged me to draw from a young age. I drew all sorts of things: lounge suites, refrigerators, lawnmowers, televisions and microwaves. These drawings were used in weekly ads for Col Buchan Discounts. His slogan was 'Where the customer is king and makes payday possible': often recited, never forgotten. Besides brochures and newspaper advertisements, I also designed paint tins and logos and directed the odd photo shoot, all before I was twenty.

At twenty-one, I secured the job of my dreams, working for *Vogue Australia*. I art-directed fashion and still life shoots and designed pages for promotions. Some of my fashion illustrations also made it on to the magazine pages. Working there was satisfying and challenging, and most importantly gave me a healthy portfolio and the confidence to set off for the other side of the world.

The Greek islands were the first stop on my travels with my lovely friend Kate. We spent two and a half months going from island to island, laughing all the way. At the end of August I arrived in cold, grey London with a suitcase of summer clothes and $1000. I had underestimated not only the weather, but also how lonely and foreign a big city could be, especially without friends. My mother wrote every week, numbering each letter. The news from home cheered me up, and her letters were brimming with love. I tried not to let my parents know how difficult life in London was, as I did not want to upset them. We all missed each other very much.

Before I left Australia, Jacquie, a *Vogue* colleague, had generously offered me her small flat in Parsons Green, suggesting I stay there until I sorted myself out. It was an absolute godsend. Several years later I bought the flat, and lived there for another ten years. It was minute: two 8-foot-wide rooms, one above the other. It also had a lovely little south-facing roof terrace, where I planted a garden and entertained in summer.

I went for interview after interview looking for a job, a soul-destroying experience. My favourite English magazine was *The World of Interiors*. It was creative and inspiring, and I wanted to work there. I contacted them and met Wendy Harrop, the art director and a pure talent. Also Australian, Wendy had travelled a similar path to London and understood the challenges I was facing. She was very complimentary and positive about my work but sadly didn't have a job for me. However, she introduced me to her husband Mel, who needed an art director for his advertising agency. I worked freelance for him, doing everything from designing brochures for hi-fi companies to directing photographs of cars in the UK and Spain.

I then spent a short time at Conran Design Group where I was senior art director for a high street fashion brand, working on all their visuals from the display material to brochures to advertising. Next was a year working in a boutique advertising agency with some lovely cosmetics and fashion clients.

My visa was about to expire and I had accepted that my work in London was coming to an end. I had started making plans to leave when I got a call from Wendy at *The World of Interiors*. She asked what I was doing and I said, 'Going home'. My parents were ecstatic that at long last I was coming back to Sydney, but Wendy was adamant she not only had the perfect job for me, as art director, but also the perfect lawyer to get me a work permit.

I immediately contacted my parents to explain I had been offered a great opportunity and would be staying in London. They cried, but they both understood just how important it was for me to fulfil my dream.

Although I'd gained a great deal from my other jobs, being at *The World of Interiors* was the first time since coming to London that I really felt connected. We were a family of like-minded people and I made strong, lasting friendships in my two and a half very happy years there. Its publisher and founder, Kevin Kelly, then asked me if I would design and art direct the British version of *W magazine*. This lovely project kept me completely occupied for a year and gave me the courage to leap into the freelance world in 1988.

I thrived as a freelance designer. I loved the freedom and diversity of my work, which spread across fashion, interiors and lifestyle. I was lucky to have an enviable list of clients and I travelled extensively. I began to explore other projects. Around the same time I picked up a Super 8 camera and started experimenting with film, which led to shooting and directing a couple of television commercials as well as doing mood films for clients. I also started buying properties, sometimes completely redesigning them. One of my most ambitious undertakings was in Clerkenwell, London. I bought the airspace on the top of a building and created a sensational 2500-square-foot apartment with two enormous wrap-around roof terraces, where I lived and worked for two and a half years. In 1998, my first book, *Sensual Living*, was published. It was an inspirational book about the senses in the home – the first of its kind.

I continued working like a maniac until 2004, when glandular fever stopped me in my tracks. During my long recuperation, I realised I no longer wanted to work in the way I had for so many years. I was getting older and my priorities were changing. There were moments when I felt a failure. Not working went against everything I believed; my life had been my work and my work had been my life. But it was time to move in a different direction. I had to muster a great deal of courage not to retreat back into the safety of what I knew. In restructuring my life, my creativity returned. The process has taken years and continues every day.

Somewhere in the midst of this journey I bought a small village house on the island of Lesvos, and now it's home. My partner Matthew Usmar Lauder, a London artist, shares and loves this new life. This book is a tribute to our life in Greece, so simple in many ways but enriched by loving animals, magnificent landscapes and wonderful people with kind faces and warm hearts.

Σπίτι μου, σπιτάκι μου

Coming home

'The isles of Greece, the isles of Greece!
Where burning Sappho loved and sung...'
                                    — Byron

When I bought my house on Lesvos, I was led by instinct – over the years I have learned to follow it without question. People always ask me how I came to be here. It was my friend Vicki who introduced me to the island; I had often told her I wanted a house away from London, a sunny place abroad. One day I said, 'I've lost my creativity; I don't feel grounded. I am terribly frustrated.'

Vicki suggested a change in direction. She held up her phone and on it was an image of a traditional stone house in a rugged landscape where fig and walnut trees stood below clear blue skies. She announced in her quiet way, 'I have bought a house in Greece on a very beautiful island.' I stared at her screen, entranced. Vicki was touched by my reaction – it felt quite profound. She said, 'Perhaps this is your remedy.' It was just up to me to take it. I phoned my friend Domenica and asked if she was up for a trip; her answer was a resounding yes.

So we set off and after a knackering all-night journey we arrived at Mytilene airport at six in the morning. Our first glimpse of Lesvos from the air was exciting: the deep blue-green Aegean Sea and a huge landmass rising from it. Dawn was breaking and warm colours streaked the horizon, a preview of the beautiful day ahead.

The sense of serenity I felt when I arrived on Lesvos was extremely powerful, and my feeling of connection to the island only grew over the hours and days of our stay. Our destination was a little hotel on a small working harbour in Molyvos. Despite being exhausted and fighting sleep, I felt so alive. I didn't want to miss anything. I was taking it all in: the smell of the sea, the warmth of the early morning air, the sound of birdsong, and the sun rising in the sky.

We followed the coastline until we entered the outskirts of Mytilene. Some of the houses were built on a grand scale, a mixture of northern and southern European architecture influenced by nearby Turkey. It was clear this place had once been very prosperous. As we continued on the road to Molyvos, the sea stretched in front of us and huge mountains rose up in the distance. We drove through all types of landscape, from dense green pine forests to salt flats where flamingos rest on their yearly migration to Africa. Colourful borders of spring flowers spilled into the surrounding fields, carpeting them in floral patterns.

Driving into Molyvos is like going back in time. Most of it sits high above sea level and the traditional stone buildings have doors, windows and shutters in a deep burnt red colour. The ruins of a Byzantine castle crown the village.

We left the car at the outskirts of the harbour and walked along its edge, where colourful fishing boats gently bobbed up and down and tourists filled the bustling tavernas and cafes. Cats and the odd dog hung around, hoping for food scraps or, better still, some affection. The locals say that if you look back towards Molyvos when departing, you will be drawn back again and again and, in some cases, never leave; the charm has certainly worked on me.

We arrived at the Sea Horse Hotel and were welcomed warmly by the proprietor, Stergios, and his wife Toula. Our simple rooms were on the second floor and had full-length shutters opening on to a small balcony with spectacular views; I would enjoy many stunning sunsets from this balcony. I used the hotel as my base once I had purchased my new house and begun renovating it. Dimitri, the owners' son, always found space for me even in the height of summer, and I was given a key during the winter months when it was closed.

I loved drifting off to sleep to the sound of glasses clinking, knives and forks against plates, chatter and laughter as people enjoyed themselves in the small restaurants below, traditional Greek music always in the background.

Often I would go out onto the balcony and watch the fishermen departing before sunrise. We waved to each other as they steered their small fishing boats out of the bay. Not long after, day broke and the swallows nesting in nearby eaves started to sing, ending the night's silence with harmony.

Domenica and I started each day with fresh fruit, Greek yoghurt, honey and nuts at a table by the harbour's edge, then headed off to explore. In the evenings we'd return for a drink before moving on to one of the local restaurants for a delicious dinner. During the week we drove all around the island and under the warm spring sunshine I decided to look for a place to live.

Finding my village was an easy accident. We left the main road and found ourselves driving down a narrow stone street edged with small houses. The village was a charming mixture of buildings, some in varying states of decay, others upright and proud with glorious gardens, fruit trees and potted flowers. It smelt of a delicious, earthy combination of food, flowers, animals and soil.

As it was spring, the main square – the heart of the village – was filled with older men, all shaded by an enormous plane tree. Some were grouped around tables playing cards and backgammon while others chatted with worry beads in their hands, drinking coffee and watching the world go by, a great Greek pastime. Samaras, a villager in his nineties, told me the tree was moved from land near the sea and planted in 1914 by a refugee. Today the main square is still *the* meeting point for young and old, all congregating under the tree. Many of them are Greeks who have ventured further afield to make new lives elsewhere, returning to see their families and connect back into village life.

We had lunch in the *kafenio* (coffee shop), a well-proportioned room with high ceilings and tall windows, filled with bright sunlight, smoke and more men, who clearly found us fascinating. A small woman with dark, wavy hair – Ralitza – greeted us warmly. She had the most beautiful, open smile and placed us in the corner of the room by a window that looked on to the street. We were presented with a variety of tasty food – far more than we could possibly eat – along with an extra dish, on the house. Ralitza is now one of my closest village friends. She and her best friend Despina have worked together in the kafenio for years, opening early and, in the busy summer months, never closing before two in the morning. They are always hospitable and jolly, looking after everyone who comes in, whether it is for a coffee, lunch, a baptism, or a name-day celebration. In that first week I had no idea what a large part Ralitza, Despina and their kafenio would come to play in my new life.

When Domenica and I finished lunch we wandered around the village taking in its charm and sizing up potential homes. Camera in hand, I snapped a few photos. I was captivated by the village; we could not have taken a better detour. Every part of me felt as if I was coming home.

Creativity suffuses everyday life
in the village - people are constantly
making lace, painting flower pots,
baking and drying herbs.
It's a very self-sufficient society -
a way of life that has worked
for thousands of years.
I often think we could learn a lot from them.

The sense of peace and calm
    pulls you in; it's profoundly restful
to sit at the water's edge and
    gaze into the vivid, intense blue.

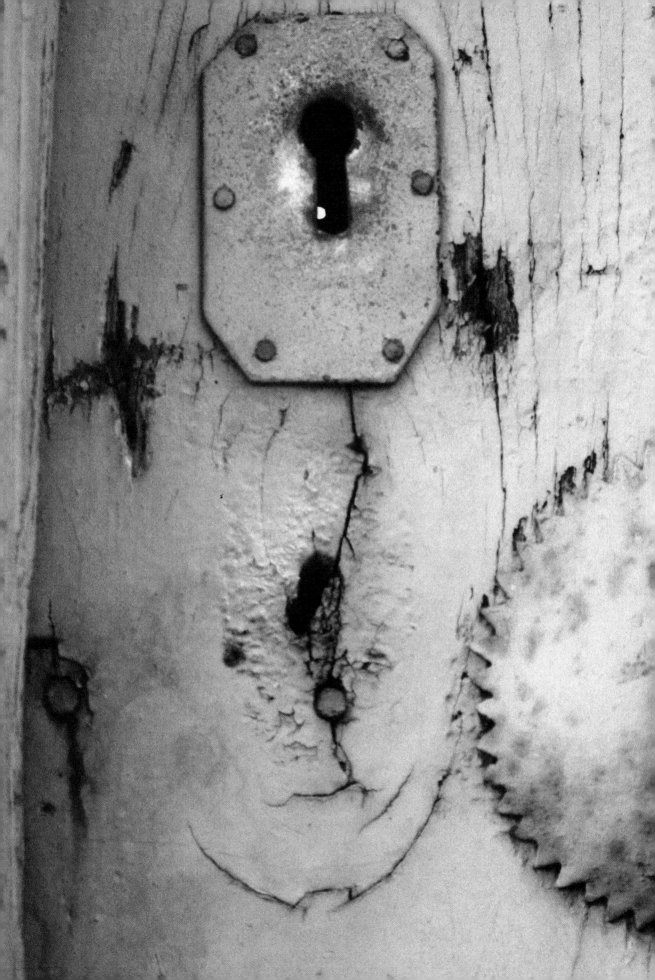

το σπίτι του Παπά

Papa's spiti

Papa's family

We engaged a local estate agent to help us look for a property; in a community such as this, word of mouth is how business is done. She was doing the rounds of the local *kafenia* (coffee shops), asking if anyone had a house they wanted to sell, when she met Gabriel, the son of the village priest, Papa. Gabriel had just returned to the village and was discussing selling his father's house with his siblings.

Papa was much loved and respected – the villagers always speak about him fondly. Buying his house seems to have given us credibility; in the beginning, when I was asked where we were staying, I would proudly reply that I had bought 'Papa's spiti' (Papa's house). The response was always an enthusiastic smile, and a warm conversation, little of which I could understand, would start. Papa came to the village in the Seventies and lived in this house until he died. His wife lived on there until she too passed away.

We met Gabriel in the *platia* (village square). Gabriel is a large-framed, polite and quiet man with a few words of English. Later, I learned that Gabriel had spent much of his life in Australia. In fact, he had married there in 1965 and had only been back to the village three times. He said that when he left the village it was a community of 3000 and was one of the largest villages in the area. It had around thirteen kafenia, but now there are just three, and a population of around 600.

Gabriel led our party – me, my friend Domenica and the estate agent – through the narrow streets and way up towards the top of the village. We reached a Turkish water fountain below an enormous *platino* (plane tree). These engraved marble water fountains, of which there are several around the village, date from the Ottoman period. The crisp, green leaves on the plane tree's long branches had just opened and this canopy provided welcome shade. Both the tree and fountain are fed by underground springs, of which there are many on the island. The villagers and their children find relief under the tree on hot summer days and gather there in the early evenings to play, chat and enjoy the spectacular sunsets. There are three of these large trees in the village and it was once a tradition to hang rope swings with wooden seats in them at Easter. On Easter Sunday when the long, elaborate Greek service had come to an end the young people would head to the tree, where they would sing, swing and flirt. The boys would push the girls high into the tree's enormous branches, the girls screaming with equal delight and horror.

Towering behind the tree was a grey, rundown house surrounded by a stone wall, a tangle of branches spilling over the top. Even in its dilapidated condition it looked large and imposing. Metal gates of a rusty, pale blue-green marked the entrance. Before passing through them we took a moment to admire the breath-taking view. A patchwork of rooftops in varying tones of terracotta spread out below us, some with their original tiles, faded and broken, others with new, clean ones. I could see the church bell tower with its clock, and out through the valley across the spring countryside. A hilly landscape of farmland divided by stone walls led all the way to the deep-blue sea, almost indistinguishable from the sky. The birds chattered noisily and continuously.

Gabriel opened the gates on to a secret, long-forgotten garden. It was quite wild and had been left to fend for itself for some time. He told me his mother had loved the garden; underneath the overgrown façade, it was still beautiful.

There were many trees and plants that, through pure determination, were still standing, starting to bloom in the spring air. Vines had wrapped like webs around the trunks of old, gnarly trees and weeds had rooted deep in the soil. The colours of the blooming flowers mixed together: shades of orange, pink and lilac combined with the different greens of weeds, shrubs and trees. Gabriel pointed proudly to all the fruit trees, the two olive trees with their beautiful silver-green leaves, the walnut tree with its fresh new growth and the enormous fig that now gives us an abundance of sun-kissed fruit each August. There was a huge old almond tree providing shade from the heat of the summer sun, and a small neat tree in the middle of the garden that produces miniature plums every June. Along with all these delights there were roses, lilac, lilies and many bearded irises. It was fantastic to see so many established plants, a great start to what would soon be my own garden.

We made our way through the chaos of the garden towards the double front door. Gabriel slowly opened one side of it, revealing a treasure trove of old family possessions. The photos on pages 32–33 will give you some idea! The house was painted in a variety of strong colours, from the deep ochre of the staircase to pink and indigo squares on the concrete floor, giving the effect of tiles. There was a lingering feeling that someone still inhabited the place; it felt full of life.

Gabriel forged upstairs with me hot on his heels. Domenica was lingering, taking in every fine detail whilst I was desperate for the full overview as quickly as possible. The stairs led up to a decent-sized landing, where a large window opened on to a view of the garden. There were two rooms, one on either side. To the right was a bedroom with another window overlooking the garden. At the opposite end was a traditional built-in cupboard that immediately caught my eye. Domenica was becoming excited about all the different fabrics lying around in piles and inside chests, particularly the handmade crocheted pieces. There was a metal bed with what looked alarmingly like a body rolled up on it. (Closer inspection revealed a wrapped bolster.)

We moved across to the room opposite, which had four windows. Gabriel struggled with their rusty catches and brilliant sunlight flooded the room as the open windows revealed views of the sea, the village and the nearest mountain. It was magnificent and at this moment I knew this house had to be mine. I have since turned the window with the view of the mountain into double doors leading out on to a roof terrace, giving us a spectacular vantage point. The mountain is crowned with a small chapel called Agios Ilias, which forms the starting point for a two-day party every July. The chapel is adorned with colourful flags and many men arrive on horseback, the horses beautifully groomed and decorated for the occasion. It is spectacular and reminds me that my instinct about this house was correct.

Following this visit, we negotiated a price and everything else went very smoothly. I was lucky to be introduced by the estate agent to a lovely Greek solicitor, Haris. He explained the contract and the whole process in detail, guided me through the paperwork and helped me set up a Greek bank account.

There was a metal bed with what
looked alarmingly like a body rolled
up on it. On closer inspection, a
wrapped bolster was revealed.

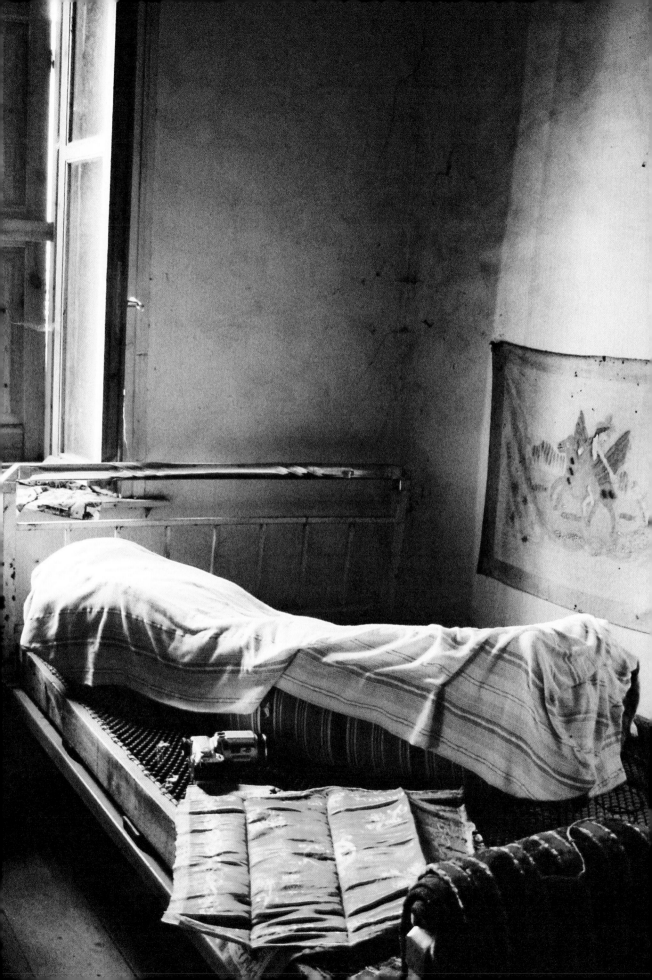

It felt as if someone was living in the house - It was full of things, from old blankets and cooking utensils to family photographs and a child's doll. I have kept as much as I could, particularly the fabrics, and use them still. Throughout the house was this vivid turquoise - the colour of the sea and the sky.

Freshly picked lilac from our garden
sits on a table made by Matthew.

After weeks of getting the paperwork together in London, the day had finally come to buy the house, amid much excitement and anticipation. Matthew had not seen it and was intrigued and amused by the fact that I could be so sure so quickly.

My niece Jessica had come from Sydney on a long-planned trip. I had promised her from the age of five that when she turned sixteen, I would bring her to London. As luck would have it, her visit coincided with our trip to Lesvos to purchase our new home. She was thrilled that a Greek island would be added to her itinerary, as she has a keen interest in Ancient Greek. Matthew, Jessica and I set out on the arduous journey that Domenica and I had first embarked upon only a month before.

The transaction had to be made in cash, the preferred currency here on the island. We met Haris at the bank in Mytilene to withdraw it before driving to Kalloni to fill out the first lot of paperwork. The actual purchase would be completed in Eressos, on the south-west of the island.

I arrived in Eressos with Haris and a bag of cash. The process seemed to take forever as the notary had many purchasers that day to deal with and a never-ending stream of people before him, all vying loudly for his attention. Everyone involved in the purchase had to be paid in cash: the notary, Haris, the agent and, of course, the family I was buying the house from. It was all very casual – the bag was opened on a table in the middle of a room filled with cigarette smoke. There was much talk (incomprehensible to me) and everyone sounded very excited.

I had left Matthew and Jessica earlier in the day to find breakfast. They dropped me off in Mytilene and were to find their own way to our destination, a restaurant in Eressos where we would celebrate with lunch, generously arranged by the estate agent. Neither Matthew nor Jessica had a clue where they were going, but to their credit, not only did they make it, they were the first to get there.

I arrived with the estate agent and Haris. Gabriel had brought along his wife and his sister Mirsini, her husband George and their grandson, and also his own son, his son's wife and his granddaughter, who were on holiday from Melbourne for the summer. The notary came along too. I was glad to have Jessica as my token relative amongst this big Greek family.

The lunch was a real treat: an abundance of delicious Greek food with lots of ouzo and *krasi* (wine). It was such a lovely way to celebrate the purchase of a new home. There was enormous enthusiasm and although we didn't speak Greek, we all joined in and enjoyed ourselves. Jessica had her first taste of the delicious local sardines, which have become her favourite dish. The lunch went on and on, a continuous stream of food: different meats and fish, crisp fresh salad, zucchini flowers stuffed with fetta, white beans in olive oil with lemon, big kidney beans in tomato sauce and much more. When it was time to leave we all felt rather stuffed, and a little too much alcohol had been consumed.

There was one last detail to attend to: the handing over of the keys. They were still back in the village, so George's grandson was sent off to collect them. He returned with a raggedy old piece of paper, which he handed over to Gabriel. The paper was slowly opened up in front of us and two old-fashioned keys — one huge and the other much smaller, held together with a piece of thread — were presented to us with a great deal of theatre, exaggerated by the amount we'd all had to drink. Finally, sixteen long hours after an exciting day had begun — a day filled with new experiences, new friends and new tastes — we were on our way back to the hotel, keys in hand and exhilarated by a sense of the life that lay ahead of us. The experience convinced Matthew that my decision to buy the house was a brilliant one, even though he still had not set eyes on it.

We started renovating right away; I was anxious to get the house ready for my parents' visit in June. Matthew and his lifelong friend Marcus worked obsessively, to the point of exhaustion, over many, many weeks to create something quirky but beautiful.

Matthew made the bed, and found the
coat hooks at the tip. The joy of life here
is having the time to learn to make many
of the things we need.

We pared back the house, painting everything white with occasional touches of the original turquoise colour, to bring out the simple beauty of each detail. Even the most ordinary objects — a stone, a shell, a pair of sandals — are worthy of attention.

Nothing is wasted—even scraps
of wood can be turned into art.

Η ζωή στο χωριό

Village life

Our friends often ask us, 'Do you think we are rich people?' Matthew's answer is always the same, 'You are very rich people; you lead rich lives.'

I never expected to live in a village – I was a city girl born and bred. I am still astounded to find myself living surrounded by rolling hills and sheep. Only recently did it dawn on me that we actually live a rural life. Matthew and I were making our way down the dirt track that leads from our house to the car park. I was dressed in white, and by the time we reached our car, I was covered in dust and fur. I turned to Matthew and said, 'We really do live in the countryside, don't we?' He laughed in disbelief and replied, 'It can't have taken you this long to realise it.'

Initially I toyed with the idea of having a house outside the village, in a more remote location. However, I am pleased we settled in a small community. Being part of the village has been rewarding and endlessly entertaining, and has also taught me how important it is to interact with people of all ages. Whether it is a simple good morning greeting of 'Kalimera', a chat about the weather, or an enquiry about where you are going or where you have been, these daily exchanges are part of the joy of village life. There is always an invitation for coffee in someone's home where the hours slip by, homemade sweets are devoured and the omnipresent television blares in the background.

The daily rituals are fascinating. Every morning at seven o'clock, a neighbour beats her rugs below our bedroom window. We can't decide whether she has an immaculate house or an obsessive-compulsive disorder. And starting at eight in the morning and continuing intermittently throughout the day, vans pass through the village, vendors bellowing their wares through loudspeakers: everything from fruit, vegetables and fish to live chicks, garden pots, plants, blankets, clothes and underwear.

When we first arrived, I spoke no Greek, so I could not understand what was being sold and would race down to the square, only to be disappointed. On one such occasion I was hoping to purchase some fruit and vegetables. I arrived outside the kafenio where a group of men were gathered around small tables. I tried to ask them where the van was but we couldn't understand each other. However, they did their best to help and one of them went into the kafenio to get the salesman. Then I saw that his van was stacked high with plastic chairs and tables; he was not selling fruit and vegetables after all. I attempted to slip away so as not to disappoint him, but I was spotted and pursued up the hill by the over-zealous salesman.

The local women gather daily in the village co-op and make cakes, biscuits, preserves and other delicious things to sell in their shop. They also make cakes and sweets for birthdays and christenings. It is clear from their chatter and laughter how much they enjoy working together. Dropping into the co-op is fascinating, particularly watching them roll small pieces of marzipan, transforming them as if by magic into delicate flowers.

And then there is Pandelis's store, where shopping can be quite an adventure, as my father discovered on his first visit. Off to buy milk, he was met by Pandelis and found himself on the back of a motorbike, heading out of town to collect fresh eggs. Over an hour later, they were spotted laughing hysterically: Dad on the back of the bike, one arm outstretched and holding a small wicker basket of fresh eggs, the other holding on to Pandelis's shoulder. What a sight!

My friend Vanessa also had the Pandelis experience when she visited. On an early morning walk, a passerby gave her a huge watermelon. Pandelis, on one of his usual trips around the village, came to her rescue – but a brief detour to have coffee with his wife Vasso had to be made before she arrived home, watermelon in hand.

The church is central to the village. On Sundays I love waking to the sound of chiming bells calling the community to prayer. The service starts at eight in the morning and is broadcast across the village. For several hours, the priest sings in his biggest and best voice, whilst various members of the congregation join in, not always in tune. The village dog, Hector, howls along from our welcome mat. Occasionally the priest also has to cover the services in other villages. Recently there was great hilarity amongst our friends because our priest was required in the neighbouring village until a replacement was found. It seems that the other priest had been defrocked and his beard shaved due to his dealings with ladies of the night. (The priest's long beard is symbolic of leaving behind secular things, as physical appearance is no longer important to him. His re-entry into the secular world is marked by the shaving of the beard.)

Easter is the most important period in the Greek religious calendar and services are held day and night, with preparations made for weeks and weeks in the run-up. On Good Friday night, young boys dressed in red robes carrying a gold crucifix lead a procession through the narrow streets. Older men follow with a shrine covered in red and white carnations. The priest stops in various spots and sings.

The procession finishes at the church, where the congregation passes underneath the elevated shrine one by one. The church is bursting with young and old, all turned out in their best. It amazes me how the women can navigate the cobbled streets in their high heels. After the service families and friends join together to celebrate and the smell of spit-roasted lamb wafts through the village.

When there is a death the church bells toll very slowly as a sign of respect. There is a small cemetery at the entrance to the village where the dead are buried, but only for a short time. After four years, the bodies are dug up, the bones are washed in wine and then wrapped in cloth and placed in small boxes decorated by their families. The boxes are stored in a building next to the graveyard.

Recently there was a lot of activity at the cemetery. It was a spring clean – everybody had to go and identify their relatives before the boxes were returned to their places on the shelves. We made our way up to the top of the cemetery and discovered a few unclaimed boxes, and a handful of people unable to find their loved ones. One woman had found her parents but could not find her uncle.

The village has a rhythm that changes with the seasons. Spring brings new life. The residents emerge from behind closed gates and open their shutters. Leaves unfold on the trees and spring flowers cover the landscape. Lambs and goats are born. Delicious edible plants are picked wild and appear in the local tavernas. It is a lovely time of year, green and filled with hope.

Summer is very hot and busy. The population of the village doubles. Relatives from as close as Athens and as far away as Canada and Australia arrive to spend July and August here. I adore the evenings when the sun slips from view, leaving wide strokes of yellow, orange, amber and purple in the sky, the final traces of the day. The temperature drops ever so slightly and the scent of flowers blends with the aroma of cooking in the night air.

We often wander down to the platia, where a delicious home-cooked meal is served under the plane tree. Young and old group together enjoying food, drink and each other's company. The energy is infectious, the buzz fantastic. The nights are long as people stay up very late. School is closed for three months and the children play into the early hours. Music drifts up to our house; I love going to sleep to the sound of people laughing and partying.

On nights when it's too hot to sleep, I drag my mattress out on to the terrace and gaze up at the sky. When I was a child, my parents would take us out in the backyard to look at the stars. I loved the Milky Way, and Mum and Dad made a bedtime game out of identifying each cluster. Here in Greece, the night sky is filled with an abundance of stars, bright and sparkling, reminding me of fairy lights.

In autumn the sun shines and it's warm enough to sit outside; even swimming in the beautiful clear sea is not out of the question. The nut trees are full and ready to be harvested. Our resident squirrels kindly help us with the collection in our garden. Pomegranates explode from the trees and also down the front of my clothes, as this delicious fruit is one of my favourites. This season my friend Fotini has given me two boxes filled with the enormous fruit, which I will juice, use in salads and eat with yoghurt. Fotini has acres of beautiful land in Sigri on the water's edge where she grows organic produce.

When winter arrives, we pile up firewood. Fruit and vegetables that have been preserved and dried throughout the year are stored. It is a time of semi-hibernation when the villagers retreat behind the thick walls of their houses and life becomes much slower and more reflective.

We have found happiness in our village. Being here has played a vital part in my self-discovery and also determined the next chapter of our lives. We feel warm, welcome and secure. Our friends have shared their traditions and given us their love.

Our lovely village house will not be transitory like others I have had. It's too special and will remain with me forever.

A delivery of winter vegetables

I am constantly struck by the way the colours
of the landscape find their way into the village.

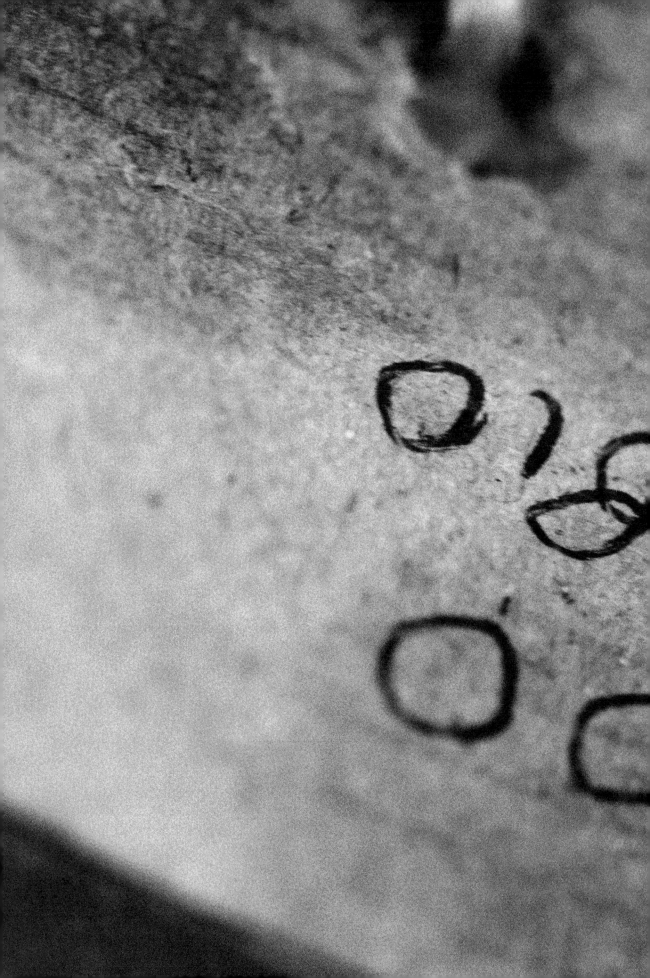

Μια καινούργια γλώσσα

A new language

Elpida

F oreign languages are not my strong point, so it was with much trepidation that I picked up the phone and dialed Elpida's number. If I wanted to communicate with these wonderful people who had welcomed me with open arms, I needed to learn their beautiful, expressive language. And how would they ever appreciate my sense of humour unless I could speak Greek? Laughter is exactly what my friends and I require as I butcher their language in my attempts to master it.

Over the years, I had tried unsuccessfully to learn another language. The first was German; on a trip to Bali I met a delicious blond, blue-eyed, tanned German surfer with a perfect muscular body. I was inspired to take up German lessons; however, these ended as the postcards and telephone calls fizzled out.

Then there was French. My close friend Gerri had moved to Paris while I was in London, and every other weekend I found myself in Paris eating, drinking, shopping, partying and generally having a high old time. I wanted to learn the language. The French lessons lasted a little longer than the German ones thanks to my very tenacious assistant, Tiffany. She explained my needs and fears to the delightful owner of a language school, who assured her that all would be fine and he had just the right person for me. After three unsuccessful meetings with three different teachers, Tiffany was fed up and insisted that I learn from the owner of the school himself. He promised he would never give up on me, but alas, this also ended in tears; as patient as he was, he eventually had to admit defeat. I didn't learn French but I discovered that I was an expert at getting my own way. Every teacher who vowed not to speak English in a quest to force me to speak French ended up losing the will to live.

Finally came Greek; this time the motivation to learn was very different. My search for a Greek teacher took some time – after a few futile attempts to find anyone to instruct me, let alone the right person, I asked Mirsini, a wonderful woman who with her husband Iannis owns the laundry in Molyvos, for advice. Mirsini suggested Elpida, who had been teaching English to her son, Andreas. She was convinced that Elpida would be perfect.

So I phoned Elpida, who laughed when I explained that I was a very frustrating student and thus far my ability for languages had proved elusive. I knew immediately by her response that she was the one and we arranged to meet. In her late thirties, Elpida is patient, intelligent, well-educated and kind. She is a classic Greek beauty like those carved into the marble porticos on ancient buildings: masses of long dark corkscrew curls frame her face, her lovely eyes are almost black, and her smile is warm and generous, just like her spirit. Elpida was born on the island and has lived in Molyvos most of her life. She studied English literature at the American College in Athens.

I love my Greek lessons and although at times I am disappointed with my progress, I know I am making headway. Sheer frustration has caused me to break down in tears: so embarrassing for a grown woman, but not surprising given my track record with languages. I am encouraged both by Elpida and also by my growing ability to read and write Greek. I try hard to keep up with my homework and although speaking is more difficult, I accept that it is going to take me time to build my confidence and my vocabulary.

Elpida and I have become close friends – and we have nights out where no Greek is spoken and I don't get home until three in the morning. This is what I have learned about the Greek language: it can sound harsh, but there is beauty in the way words are put together. It is very descriptive and also quite literal – for example 'hotel' is *ksenothohio*; literally, 'stranger container'; 'post office' is *tahithromio*, meaning 'fast service', which is never the case, and 'rose' is the very beautiful *triantafillo*: thirty petals.

The more I hear, the more I learn, the more I understand, the more committed I am to speaking Greek fluently. So I continue *siga siga* – slowly, slowly.

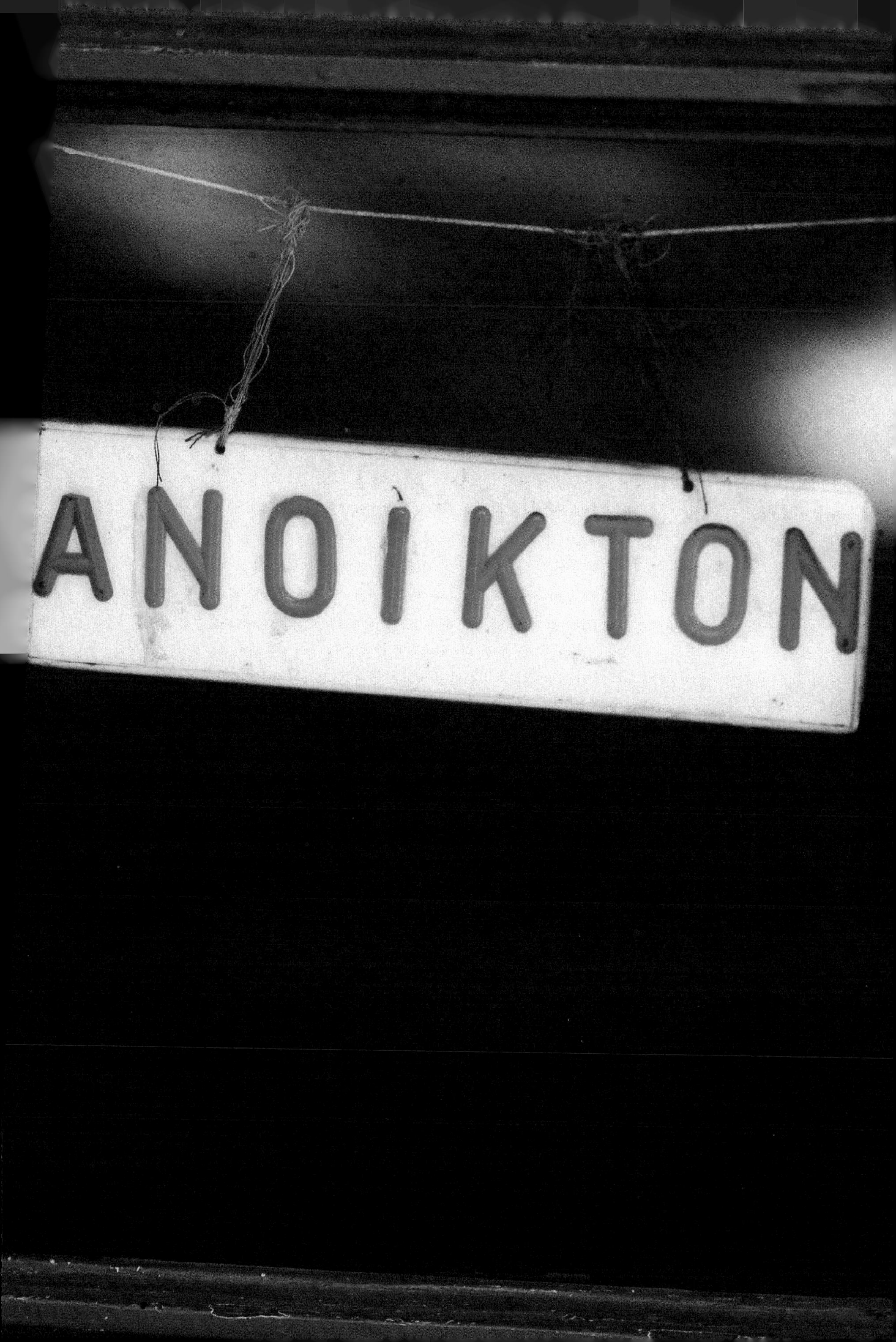
ΑΝΟΙΚΤΟΝ

Άγρια σπαράγγια

Asparagus hunt

Pandelis

After one of my early morning walks, I came back to find our house deserted and the front door wide open. There was no sign of Matthew, but in the kitchen I found the abandoned remains of his half-eaten breakfast. Matthew never lets anything distract him from eating, so whatever had lured him away must have been important.

It was nearing lunchtime; I was about to prepare one of my favourite simple salads made with walnuts from the garden, a neighbour's pomegranates and locally grown lettuce. I couldn't think where Matthew might be, so I texted him to see if he wanted to join me for lunch. He responded immediately, saying that he was indeed really hungry and had been hijacked by Pandelis several hours earlier, but would be returning soon. Little did he know . . .

Pandelis, who owns a small mini-market in our village, has been a good friend and often includes us in his family events. In his mid-fifties, he has curling, greying hair, a stocky build and an intense stare that can make him seem surly. He can be moody, but also often dissolves into hysterical laughter. He works hard on his land and is generous with his produce, often bringing us eggs and goat milk. His English is good, due to the time he has spent in Canada.

Pandelis had climbed the steep hill from his house to ask Matthew to pick wild asparagus with him. Pandelis is not the kind of man you say no to, so off Matthew went. What started out as a trip in search of wild asparagus turned into an odyssey, and it was dusk by the time Matthew finally made it home, exhausted, ravenous and covered in sweat, dirt and blue dye. Only then did I hear the full story.

Matthew had just made his coffee and toast when Pandelis arrived as if from nowhere and explained that they would go asparagus picking after they had collected some stones from the side of the road for a house he was planning to build.

The idea was that Pandelis would drive his pick-up truck along the road and Matthew would leap out and pick up the stones, which, as the journey went on, increased dramatically in size. As the stones turned to large rocks, Pandelis started to look worried, perhaps fearing that despite Matthew's size (he is six foot two), he wasn't up to the job after all. Matthew was panicking too, thinking about his back and the recent hours of physiotherapy sessions he had endured. However, he was not to be outdone by the village alpha male. Knowing Matthew as I do, I imagine that, despite his concerns, he would have undertaken this strenuous work with one of his huge wrap-around smiles reaching almost behind his ears.

Pandelis, not satisfied with what had already been collected from the designated piles at the side of the road, drove into the dusty countryside to pick up even bigger rocks. Matthew found it hard to believe the strength of this man who was ten years his senior. Some of the rocks were so enormous that it took both of them to get them into the truck. And to add to the experience, as Pandelis picked up one of the rocks hundreds of large, black, biting ants transported themselves on to his sweater. He did a cursory brushing-off, but showed no sign of panic. Matthew told me that Pandelis seemed almost comfortable covered in these big black biters.

After unloading the rocks from the truck it was time to move on to the search for wild asparagus. This is a difficult task for a newcomer and it took Matthew almost twenty minutes to learn to recognise them. Wild asparagus grow sparsely on spiky bushes. There are two different types, each with a different culinary use. The leafier one is used in a watery soup which is both oily and vinegary. It is not a huge favourite of mine. More to my taste is the less leafy variety, which is prepared in a frying pan with eggs and oil to create a delicious dish, *omeleta me sparaggia* (asparagus omelette).

The asparagus season only lasts a few weeks, so the picking was driven by a sense of urgency; Matthew felt as if it would never end. The two men had started at the coast and worked their way inland, filling three carrier bags with fresh asparagus as they went. This took three solid hours. As each bag was filled Matthew was certain the job was done but no, out came another bag. With the third bag full to the brim, Matthew, exhausted and near-delirious with hunger, was finally on his way home, or so he thought. As they neared the village, Pandelis stopped the truck again and announced that the sheep (which live in one of Pandelis's fields along with a cat, five kittens and a handful of chickens) needed to be fed.

This done, their work was still not over for the day. Next the goats and their newborn kids needed taking care of. Each night, for the first two weeks of their lives, all the babies have to be put safely into a manger with straw insulation to protect them from cold and foxes. Two babies had been born that morning and what was left of their umbilical cords had to be sprayed with a blue disinfectant dye. Matthew cradled them in his arms rather than the more usual method of dangling them by their two front legs, which might have been more humane, but meant the blue dye not only met its target, but covered Matthew too. Finally, after the longest of days, they got back in the truck again and this time headed for the village.

Seven hours after he had left the house, an exhausted, hungry and traumatised Matthew stood before me, delivering Pandelis's invitation to an asparagus feast, to be presented in the local taverna in under two hours' time. A huge amount of wild asparagus was served as a soup first, and then in the omeleta me sparaggia for the second course. While the food was gratefully received by all, there was a palpable sense of anti-climax in the air, despite the accompanying ouzo. Both Pandelis and Matthew were physically exhausted by the exertions of the great asparagus hunt and boulder-shifting exercise. Not only that, their conversation had probably peaked several hours earlier.

I have given the recipe for omeleta me sparaggia overleaf – it is very simple to make, but extremely delicious.

Omeleta me sparaggia

This wild asparagus dish looks rather untidy, but it's absolutely delicious. Put it on the table with a large spoon for people to help themselves.

Bring a saucepan of water to the boil. Snap the woody bases from the asparagus and discard, then break the asparagus into pieces approximately 4 cm long. Drop the asparagus pieces into the water and boil for 2–3 minutes, until just tender, then remove from the water and drain in a colander.

Heat a medium-sized non-stick frying pan over a high heat, add olive oil, then add the asparagus to the pan. Pour the eggs over the top and cook, uncovered, for 4–5 minutes until just set. Slide out on to a plate, scatter the crumbled fetta over the top, season with salt and pepper and serve

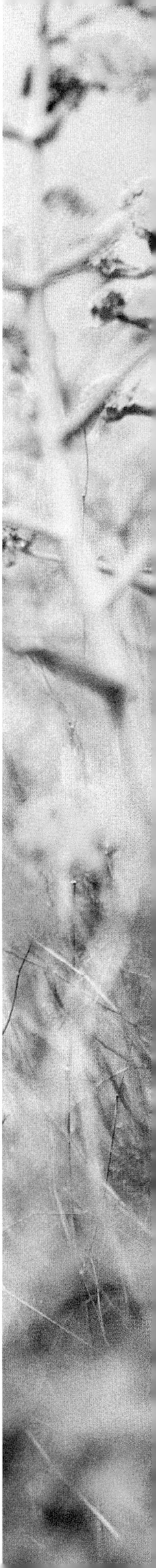

**Serves 6
as part of a shared meal**

340 g wild or thin cultivated asparagus

olive oil for frying

6 eggs, beaten

200 g fetta cheese, crumbled

salt and freshly ground black pepper

Καψενεία

Kafenia

stratos

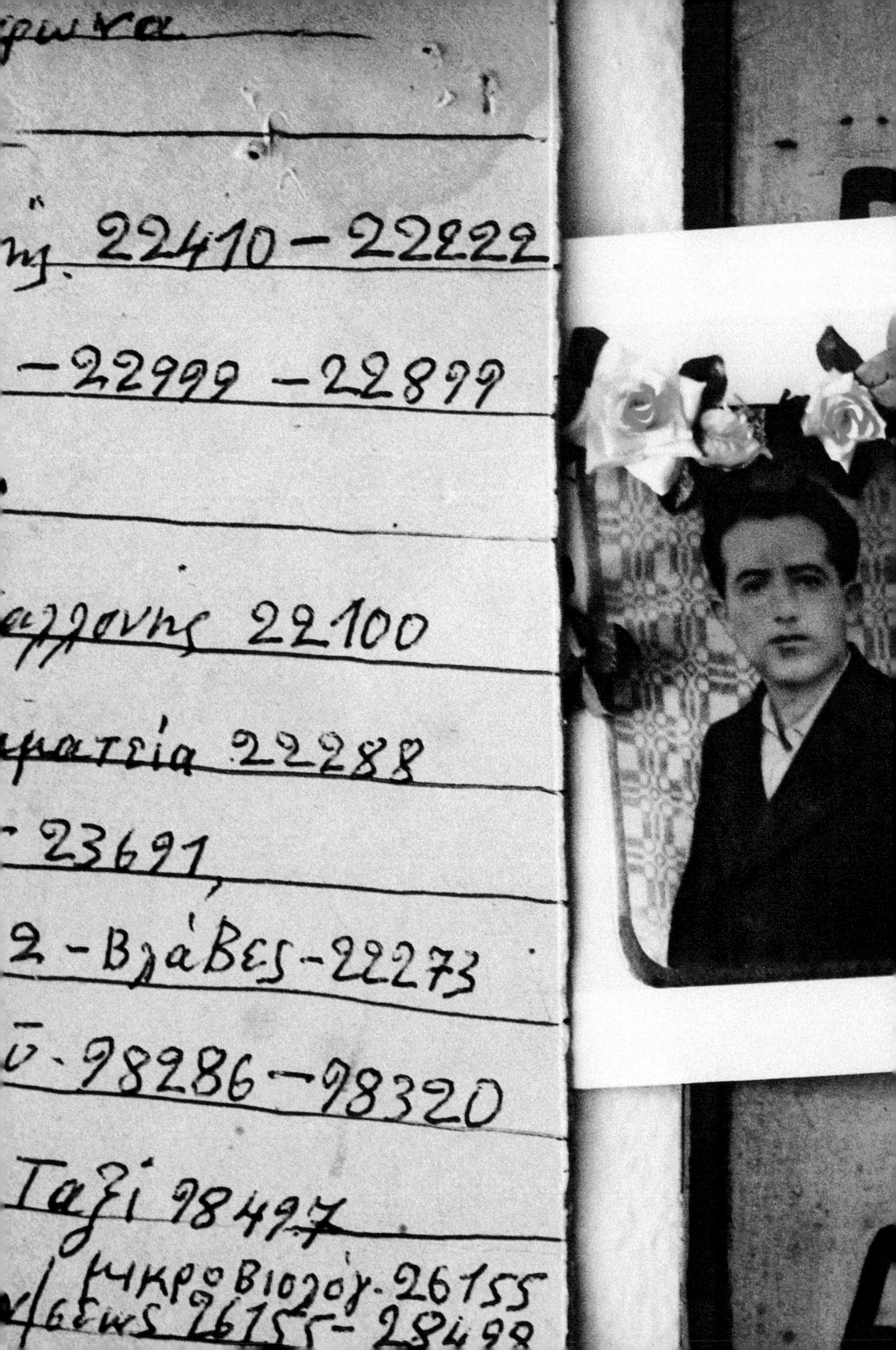

ρινα

" η. 22410 - 22222

- 22999 - 22899

αγγουης 22100

ματεία 22288

- 23691

2 - Βλάβες - 22273

ῦ. 98286 - 98320

Ταξί 98497

Μικροβιολογ. 26155

ήσεως 26155 - 28498

This cafe feels timeless; nothing ever changes there.

Panayiota

Ralitza

Over eight very long weeks in winter, Matthew and our friend Marcus applied coat after coat of bright white paint to the walls, ceilings and doors of our new home. Most evenings after working on the house, they ate dinner at one of the two kafenia, which are opposite each other in the village. One is owned by an older couple, Stratos and Panayiota, while the other is owned by Ralitza and Despina. The boys were usually exhausted after working on the house in ten-hour stretches, and very grateful to have someone else prepare their meals.

Stratos and Panayiota's kafenio is the more traditional, with lovely old wooden chairs and tables. It is quiet and intimate with a small menu, and is by far the most characterful and charming venue in the village. It is also where the couple live, which makes it easy for Stratos to slip upstairs in the middle of the day for a nap. Panayiota stays downstairs watching soap operas on a small television perched on the back wall, interrupted by the occasional customer.

Matthew and Marcus could be found here twice a day sipping *café ellenikas*, the strong, sweet Greek coffee that kept them going until dinnertime. Often Stratos would go to the freezer and select something (frozen rock-solid) and then discuss how he and Panayiota would prepare it for the evening meal as they drank their coffee. He often became very animated, excited by the potential of the food to be cooked.

On the nights that Marcus and Matthew ate at Stratos and Panayiota's, they were often the only customers. The boys were always well looked after and being there reminded them of their grandparents' houses, though here there was a bill at the end of the meal.

Stratos loves an audience and he would talk to Marcus and Matthew in Greek, German, Spanish and Italian, sometimes all in the same sentence. Stratos particularly favours German, as he once worked in Germany as a hairdresser. Occasionally the kafenio doubles as the village barber shop. It is not uncommon to find Stratos by the chest freezer wielding a pair of scissors, towel draped over the shoulders of a local man.

Matthew and Marcus asked Stratos to cut their neglected hair. He was delighted but rather than do it by the freezer he took them upstairs to the flat where he and Panayiota live. The couple's possessions and photos of them when they were young adorn the flat, filling it with an intriguing atmosphere.

Into a bedroom they went where scissors, clippers, combs and a cut-throat razor lay on a table. Stratos began with Matthew, using a pair of clippers that looked as if they'd been made in the Sixties. Although slow and a bit shaky, Stratos definitely knew what he was doing, though Matthew did worry when the clippers were swapped for the razor. The boys emerged from the kafenio looking much more presentable, give or take the odd protruding hair.

Across the street, dinner at Ralitza and Despina's kafenio is a completely different experience. Hectic and buzzy most nights, the restaurant is often filled with men sharing a meal or playing cards, and there is always a table or two with a lone man looking on, watching the game. Friendly banter flies constantly between the tables, and on weekends and during the busy summer period, women and children join the crowd. If the large wall-mounted television in the corner is not switched on, traditional Greek music plays loudly. In summer, the action spills on to the pavement where every available bit of space is taken up with tables. No two nights are ever the same.

In the winter months, the men of the village convene around a makeshift stove in the centre of the restaurant. In Stratos and Panayiota's place it is a salvaged oil drum fitted with an enormous funnel-type chimney that directs the smoke (or most of it) out of a window at the front of the restaurant. In Ralitza and Despina's kafenio the stove is a little more sophisticated, adding to the warm atmosphere.

It was in the kafenia that Matthew and Marcus really bonded with the locals. They would sit around a communal table and share food: the more people, the more food, the cheaper the evening. It is not unusual for someone to come in with a pig, slaughtered that day, and hand it over to the kitchen to be cooked and served at dinner. Sometimes Ralitza makes a surprise pudding and generously serves it to everyone at the end of a meal.

One evening George, a small, gentle, blond-haired farmer, wearing his trademark bright blue overalls, rose from the table and began a dance the Greeks call *zeibekiko*, 'the drunken dance'. When he had finished, he simply sat down and continued eating. Just one of many wonderfully spontaneous moments we have witnessed at both kafenia.

There are so many characters that make the kafenia memorable. One of them is Kosta, an old man with one blind eye. He makes a little extra money fetching cigarettes for the other diners from a small shop just a stone's throw away. He is the butt of some of the men's jokes but he simply laughs, taking it all in his stride.

There are also the Chinese travellers, who arrive in the village throughout the year. They come in a car laden with their wares: anything from dishcloths, hand-held fans and knives to cigarette lighters with naughty pictures on them and singing plastic birds on stands. They always elicit much amusement. An ordinary evening becomes an eventful one – all the men join in, laughing and testing out the imported bits and pieces.

Cafe culture is essential to the Greek way of life; for many people the kafenio is a second living room, where they while away hours exchanging news or engaging in spirited debate about the state of the world, playing cards or backgammon, or reading the newspaper. More than simply a place to eat, it is perhaps the modern equivalent of the *agora* – the public arena of ancient Greece where philosophers and orators would discuss their theories on life and hawkers would peddle their wares among a heaving, jostling, joyously noisy crowd.

Chavalambos

Cafe society on the island. The kafenia are the social hub of the village, and the number of visitors fluctuates with the seasons. In the summer they teem with life; in the winter it's just the village regulars exchanging news, having their fortunes read in the coffee grounds or just contemplating the meaning of life.

Τα λουλούδια της Ειρήνης

Irene's loulouthia

One morning I was up and out early, before seven. My aim was to get back before nine to embark on the day's chores. Off I went with our dogs Hector and Mutters – the usual morning dog madness, both of them in a state of great excitement.

On my return I ran into one of my neighbours, Irene. She is a small, handsome woman in her late sixties with salt-and-pepper hair. As a widow, she lives alone, but she is very sociable; she has a warm smile, an animated manner and a unique sense of style. She insists on speaking to me very, very slowly in Greek, sometimes almost in a whisper. When my eyes glaze over she grabs me by the arm, looks me in the eye and repeats herself several times; she has enormous patience. I believe she thinks I understand much more than I do, but her method of communicating is still good. I'm certain that if I could spend more time with her my Greek would advance far more quickly.

A large ball of cotton wool under a huge white bandage concealed half of her face. Irene explained that she had been by the sea (*thalassa*) when she fell, banged her head and cut herself under the eye, meaning a trip to the hospital in Mytilene for a scan and stitches. I was able to understand this much! She looked black and blue, but was still friendly and cheerful.

She directed me to her zucchini vine and instructed me to pick the big yellow trumpet-shaped flowers covering it. In Greek these flowers are called *loulouthia*. They are delicious and there are several ways to cook them. She guided me to different parts of the vine, pointing towards the flowers she wanted me to pick; we then headed to her kitchen. Above the sink the end of a chrome tap had been neatly covered in a pink net fabric. I believe this is a simple way of filtering the water – it looks superb.

Beautiful crocheted fringes made by Irene's mother edged the shelves of a green marbled formica cupboard, and a line of jars behind the sink were filled with hand-picked herbs. There was also a huge bunch of mint, fresh from the garden, in a blue plastic basket balanced on a chair. Decorating the exterior window ledges of this much-used blue, green and yellow kitchen were small green bottles of pussy willow.

Irene pulled some fetta out of the refrigerator and started pointing to various bowls and plates on different shelves, all much too high for her to reach. I fetched them for her on tiptoe, as I am not actually much taller than she is. Meanwhile other ingredients started to appear one by one: eggs, flour and the mint. As she started cutting up the leaves, it dawned on me that she was about to cook for me, so I rushed back to the house to grab my camera. I was closely followed by Hector, who had been waiting for me outside the gauze door, not missing a trick. At one point Irene opened the door and hurled a bit of cheese his way, surprising both him and me.

I am always struck by the generosity and spontaneity of these people. It is refreshing; such a contrast to rigid city life. I still have to remind myself to enjoy the moment and not worry if things don't turn out as planned.

Camera in hand, I started to photograph the making of these wonderful fritters. The flowers and herbs were chopped, and the fresh eggs and plain flour added. Irene then reached for an ouzo bottle and poured a small amount into the bowl. 'Ouzo?' I asked, but she shook her head: 'Nero'. It's mineral-rich water collected from a nearby spring, which she stores in a glass bottle to help keep the flavour.

Once the batter is mixed, it is dropped into sizzling olive oil in a frying pan a spoonful at a time; it doesn't take long for the fritters to be ready. Irene arranged them on a red plastic plate and beckoned me into the main house, where we chatted as we ate. There were some fantastic photographs hanging on Irene's walls and as she began to tell me who was who, I felt honoured to be allowed such insight into her life. By the time Hector and I took our leave it was nearly eleven o'clock, almost four hours since we had set off. I left feeling grateful for such an unexpected and intimate experience with another village friend.

Irene makes her loulouthia fritters.
I love the varied and
complementary green colours in
her kitchen. The lace tablecloth
and doilies were made by Irene's
mother — beauty is literally woven
into the fabric of everyday life here.

Irene's loulouthia fritters

These fritters are best eaten as soon as you make them, crisp and fresh from the pan. You can drain them on some kitchen paper first for a few seconds if you find them too oily. They are a great example of the way the Greeks find a way to use every edible part of a plant, even flowers.

Place cheese in a mixing bowl and season with pepper. Add eggs, chopped flowers, mint and flour and mix well. If necessary, add a small amount of water (just enough to bind the mixture together). Heat a non-stick frying pan, add a splash of olive oil, then drop in tablespoons of the mixture. Don't overcrowd the pan. Cook fritters until golden brown (approximately 4–5 minutes each side). Drain on kitchen paper and serve.

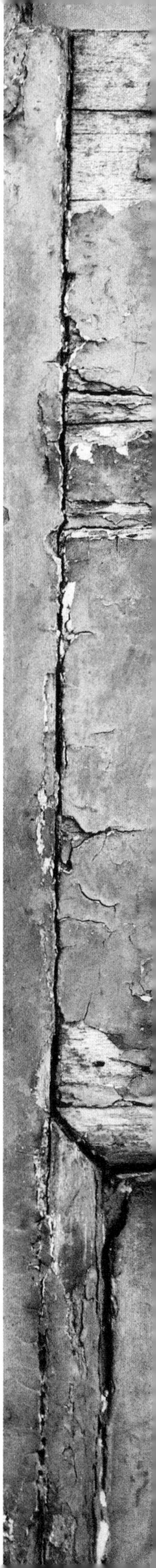

Serves 2

100 g fetta cheese, crumbled

freshly ground black pepper to taste

2 eggs, beaten

15 zucchini flowers, roughly chopped

¼ cup chopped fresh mint leaves

50 g plain flour (approximately)

water

olive oil for frying

Το σπίτι του Κεν

Ken's spiti

At the upper entrance to the village are two small, adjoining houses which were derelict when we first came to the village. One had had some work done on it before being abandoned a few years ago; the other was untouched. The houses are mirror images of one another, and in a perfect spot for watching the sunset as they have uninterrupted views straight to the sea.

I had admired these houses on many occasions. One of our neighbours, Effie, mentioned that the untouched house was for sale – it belonged to her family. She explained that they had been built for the two oldest of five sisters. Effie's cousin Efrocine, the youngest, had been sent to the Convent of the Virgin of Myrsiniotisis in Kalloni at the age of five to stay with her godmother, and has lived there ever since. Now, sixty-odd years later, she was charged with the sale of the family house. When I told Effie that we might be interested in buying it, we were whisked off (my parents, who were staying with us, included) to the convent to meet Efrocine and discuss the purchase.

We arrived in the late afternoon. Effie showed us the convent's various chapels and buildings and took us through the lush gardens. She explained that the few aged nuns who still live here tend the gardens and take it in turns to hold a continuous vigil of prayer in the main chapel. It was a very warm day; we sat under the shade of a tree and were offered coffee. Effie was the go-between and translated for us in her gravelly voice, rough from years of chain smoking. Her husband Nick sat beside her, making us laugh with his cheeky sense of humour.

My father was in his element, as he has always been partial to nuns. Many of our Sunday excursions during my childhood would be derailed because my father, the 'nun-spotter' as we called him, had seen a nun (or nuns) waiting at a bus stop. My father would stop the car and squeeze her (or them) into the back seat next to my two siblings and me. He would then deposit the nun (or nuns) safely at her (or their) destination – even if it happened to be in the opposite direction from where we were headed.

Efrocine returned carrying a tray laden with cups and a bowl overflowing with Turkish delight. We scoffed the sweets, although Effie preferred to puff her way through a box of thin white cigarettes. The bowl was seriously depleted by the time it was whisked away.

Efrocine shared stories about the lovely times she had spent at the house with her family. After reminiscing, she was anxious to know if our intentions were serious. I promised to let her know the following morning. Just before we left my father asked, 'Sister, please pray tonight for my daughter to make the right decision about the house.' I can only guess what she prayed for! I suspect Sister needed a good lie-down after our departure.

Our decision was a resounding 'Yes' and we named the house 'Ken's Spiti' after my father. Efrocine came to see it one last time before we began working on it, and also took the opportunity to visit her mother's grave in the village cemetery. She described what the house and the village were like when she was a child, then took a few pieces of memorabilia: a simple oil lamp and a little vase, which I had secretly coveted but of course it was right that she should have them. She said she'd like to return once the work was done, and one day I hope she will.

My friend Victoria introduced us to Alex, a fun, efficient Italian woman who would oversee the building work. Through Alex we met Yiannis, a reliable builder who takes a craftsman's approach to his work.

The tiny house originally consisted of an entrance hall, a very small kitchen with a fireplace, and two small interconnecting rooms, all on one floor. There was plenty of space under the house, however, so we decided to excavate and create a lower level.

Yiannis and his team worked hard for months and the fruit of their labours is simple and stunning. This house serves mainly as our guesthouse, a perfect place for family and friends to stay.

Soft, warm afternoon light fills the house
with a sense of peace and calm.

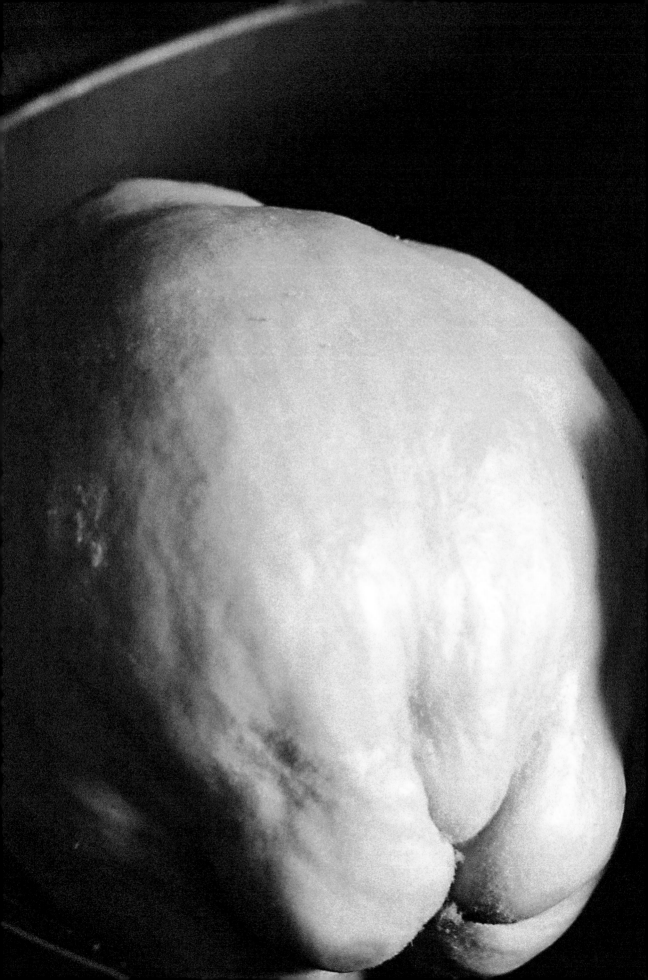

Το γλυκό κυδώνι της γιαγιάς

Yiayia's quince spoon sweet

Yiayia

My friend Konstantina phoned to ask if Matthew and I would like to join her and her new husband Apostolis, for lunch in their apartment in Mytilene. Matthew and I had attended their wedding a few months previously, as well as visiting the house before the ceremony to witness the bride and groom preparing themselves. Today's lunch would be the first meal Konstantina would cook for guests as a married woman.

Konstantina had arranged for us to stop at her grandmother's house before lunch. Yiayia (as the Greeks call their grandmothers) had offered to cook her quince *glyko tou koutaliou* ('spoon sweet') for me; this traditional sweet can be made using a variety of fruits or vegetables, including cherries, tomatoes and even marrow. It was all very relaxed as we gathered in the kitchen chatting, laughing and helping. Yiayia peeled and grated the quinces, then soaked them in water with lemon juice. Konstantina and I went into the garden to pick *amparoriza*, a lemon-scented geranium used as a flavouring.

Yiayia washed and dried as she went, keeping the kitchen tidy, while Matthew and Apostolis helped to skin and chop the almonds. The men, both towering head and shoulders above Yiayia, were also the first to taste the sweet treat as she delighted in spooning it into their mouths.

It is said that to cook sweet food you must first have sweet thoughts, and watching Konstantina's grandmother at work in her kitchen being helped by family members, I certainly had plenty of these. It is a room that brims with sweet thoughts, generous hospitality and love. We all went off to lunch at Konstantina's in high spirits.

Glyko tou koutaliou

I have given quantities to produce enough to fill
a 1-litre jar, but if you have your own tree, simply
adjust the proportions to match the weight of quinces
you want to preserve. The delicate lemon fragrance of
this sweet comes from the amparoriza; it enhances the
flavour of the quince. If you can't find it, lemon-scented
geranium, lemon verbena or lemongrass will give
a similar result.

Peel and grate the quinces into a bowl, sprinkling with lemon
juice and water as you go. Once all the quinces are peeled and
grated, remove them from the lemon and water, squeeze out the
excess liquid and put them in a large saucepan. Add the sugar,
enough water to cover the quinces, and all other ingredients,
and mix well. Bring gently to the boil over a medium heat,
then simmer over low heat, stirring regularly to prevent catching,
until the quince is tender and the syrup is thick – usually
2–3 hours. Test the consistency by pouring a dessertspoon
of syrup on to a plate – when it sets easily, it is ready.

Makes 1 litre

1 kg quince, peeled and grated
juice of half a lemon
1 kg sugar
500 g almonds, blanched, peeled and chopped
a handful of whole amparoriza leaves
1 tsp citric acid (*lemontouzo*)

Πρωίνοι Περίπατοι

Morning walks

M

y morning walks have developed into something of a ritual, albeit a chaotic one. Depending on the season, these outings begin as early as six o'clock, and I usually walk for about seven kilometres. I head out of the village along a very dusty, uneven rocky road sheltered by a canopy of green pine trees that provide wonderful relief from the scorching mid-summer sun. In the winter I collect their enormous, full cones to burn in our fire, so the smell of pine fills our cosy house.

I walk towards the sea; most of this part of the walk is downhill, making it far less challenging than the return leg. The Aegean Sea is directly ahead of me and depending on the time of year and the weather conditions its colour varies from a very deep blue through to one that's much lighter. When it's windy, the still water is transformed into white peaks. To my right is the north of the island and in the distance, Turkey. It is hard to believe just how close we are to Turkey – we are only separated by a small amount of water; in places this can be as little as 5 kilometres across.

In this ancient landscape I get a sense of wisdom from every tree and every rock. I often wonder about the people who have worked the land for centuries. What kinds of lives they led; how connected they must have been to nature, as they would have relied on it so strongly to survive. There is still a sense of that today.

Springtime provides an abundance of colourful wild flowers paving the dirt track and spilling into and carpeting the fields. Poppies, daisies, wild crocus, dandelions, cornflowers, thistles and chamomile produce a wonderful confusion of reds, blues, pinks, purples and yellows. They all sit side-by-side but each

Turkey —
a stone's throw away

stands alone in its beauty. I often pick armfuls of flowers to place around our house. I love this time of year for its freshness and renewed life; there is always a feeling of hope. There are many olive and acorn trees and the farm animals are well camouflaged, blending into the dusty landscape.

The harsh summer days leave the track dusty and the surrounding fields and farms dry. Relief in the landscape comes from clusters of oleander trees with coloured flowers ranging from whites through to pinks and oranges. They cluster in areas where they can draw water from the underground springs that flow deep beneath the earth throughout the year. There are also a large number of rocks covered in lichen that changes dramatically depending on the season and the amount of light and rain. After heavy rainfall the rocks take on a very strong presence in the landscape. Their surfaces darken and their form is much more prominent, accentuated by the lichen.

Autumn days are usually clear and crisp with the leaves changing to beautiful golds and reds before they fall. The air is still warm, the sun gives out the last of its strength, and there is usually a light breeze. My enthusiasm for walking is renewed as the exhaustion from the summer heat slowly dissipates. And by the time winter reaches us there is a palpable shift towards hibernation. The villagers disappear behind their gates and shutters into the comfort of their homes.

Winter can be as harsh as summer. Sometimes the clouds are so low you can't see two feet ahead of you. It can be bitterly cold, and snow is not out of the question. High winds can make walking nearly impossible. If the wind is behind you, you can be pushed so hard that there is no need for any effort, however if the wind is head-on, moving at all can prove virtually impossible. I love the change in the seasons and with it the change of landscape.

Matthew has started walking with me and we have a few friends who also come along. There is Nellie, our lovely but incredibly nervous dog. She lurches from a broad smile of delight to a 'please don't beat me' look within seconds. We found her secured to a fence on roughly a metre of chain; she was malnourished and her whole body was badly affected. She was terribly thin, her coat was coarse and there was no fur whatsoever around her neck, where the chain had rubbed the fur down to her bare skin. Fleas and ticks hung off her, virtually sucking the life from her. Her back was hunched and her paws spread wide due to her confinement and lack of exercise. She is

a tan and white, medium-sized dog with no tail. Nellie has big, round, kind eyes accentuated by markings that look like eyeliner.

The second friend who joins us is Hector, the village dog. I believe he was dumped at the edge of the village and has had to survive using his cunning, along with his enormous personality. Nellie, Matthew and I leave the house and Hector is often waiting outside the front gate in anticipation. He always gives us a warm welcome and is equally excited to see Nellie, who he clearly has the glad eye for. Hector leads the way, constantly looking behind with his beady little eyes to make sure we are all keeping up. He has a couple of unfortunate habits: one is chasing cats, the other chasing cars. Hector is very fast and rounding up the cats is a great game to him, but a nail-biting experience for both the cats and us. If the cat takes off, so does Hector and no amount of shouting at the top of our voices will deter him. Matthew and I turn into two screaming banshees so quickly it's frightening. A lovely peaceful walk turns into an uncontrollable yelling fiasco. Hector always turns back and looks at us so proudly. When he races off, his back legs leave the ground at the same time, swinging from one side to the other – the result of many car-chasing incidents.

Hector's perilous car-chasing sets my adrenaline going and makes my heart pound, making climbing the hills a double workout. If we hear a car coming we run towards him – if we are fast enough we grab him by the scruff of the neck before he lurches, barking madly, in front of the wheels. Otherwise we just have to watch as he hides, squatting down low at the side of the road, camouflaged and ready to attack the front wheels of the approaching enemy. The screaming starts up once again as, hoarse and breathless, we worry that those being attacked will be thinking we should control our dog. Those who know Hector is the village dog are not deterred and just keep driving, considering us crazy for getting involved. It is the tourists who make me most nervous. In their attempt to avoid Hector's madness they could so easily skid off the edge of the road, down a 30-foot cliff on to the rocks below. Oblivious to their plight, I'm sure Hector would then just look up at us proudly, having saved us from the enemy. Red cars and trucks are a particular threat.

We have named the latest addition to our crew Muttley (or Mutters), and he bears a remarkable resemblance to Hector. Matthew and I are convinced that he is Hector's offspring. He is short with lots of tan fur and a tail like Hector's.

He is a puppy really, with all the playfulness and mischief that goes with it. Kyriakos, his owner, is quite happy for us to take Muttley with us when we go on our walks and it's a good opportunity for him to run fast and free. We collect him last. We have to cross a field and walk down a hill to where he is chained beside the chicken coop. He sees us coming well before we arrive and lets us know with a high-pitched bark that he is not to be forgotten. Muttley has usually almost choked himself, frantically pulling on his chain, by the time we reach him. He is anxious to be untied, but we are aware that he will waste no time heading for his playmates the chickens, and one will instantly be pinned to the ground. We arrive dog lead in hand and hope we can make the changeover quickly enough to avoid a chicken episode.

Off we all go along the track, Hector ahead and on high alert. Nellie stays beside us, constantly looking up at us for approval. Once the sound of a distant shot could send her running into the fields without looking back, causing us hours of anxiety while we searched for her. She is getting much better the more time she spends with us and with every walk she gains slightly more confidence.

Being a puppy, Muttley thinks everything is a game, hurling himself up and down rocks and at both Nellie and Hector. He also bites at our feet and pulls at our laces, a hugely annoying habit when we're trying to walk. He goes at such a pace that he skids before coming to a stop, sending clouds of dust and small rocks in all directions. You can hear his panting breath get louder as he approaches from behind. When Hector has had enough of Muttley's hurling antics he pulls rank, bares his teeth and coralls him into a ditch on the side of the path. There he forces him to stay until he sees fit to allow him back into the pack. Matthew and I hope that the day's quota of red cars and trucks will pass while Hector is occupied putting Muttley in his place. These walks are not the most relaxing start to the day, but we love them just the same.

We have begun to expect the unexpected on these excursions. Recently I came around a bend in the road to find an old chair hanging high in one of the acorn trees. I really could not understand why. It looked rather good, as if it had been placed there for a magazine shoot – not unlike something I would have set up in the past. The angle I approached it from was stunning: a dirt road led towards the tree and beyond it in the distance the countryside rolled down to the deep blue water, a brilliant azure sky overhead. It took me several days to find out why the chair was there. Gregory, a man who has recently come back to the village after living most of his life in South Africa, told me that he keeps the chair in that spot as it is a beautiful place to stop and enjoy the view. He has also made a wooden bird, which he has placed on top of the tree to show the direction of the wind. The bird is painted white; it has been crudely cut out and wide brushstrokes of red and blue stretch horizontally along its wings, resembling feathers. A handmade wooden propeller turns it with the wind, and it is attached to the tree by a length of what looks like a wooden broom handle, painted blue. It is so charming and a little like outsider art.

Gregory has a very strong and energetic young golden retriever called Pepe. He walks Pepe everyday; Pepe is so keen to make friends he can actually knock you to the ground with his enthusiasm. He loves seeing me and I think would like to join our gang. I always stop for a stroke and a chat, much to the annoyance of Team Hector. Hector gives a low growl under his breath, Muttley keeps his distance and Nellie does an extraordinary whimper which builds up to a bark — a jealous performance on her part. Nellie otherwise only does this in the car when we pass a donkey; for some unfathomable reason she lets out a single bark.

Further along the track there are a couple of waterholes, one on the road and one on an adjacent farm. When they are filled with water, they teem with frogs that plop loudly into the water as Team Hector approaches. The waterhole on the farm lasts longer than the one on the road, which disappears as the weather gets warmer. This confuses Muttley and sends him in search of it. The farm waterhole is in a much more picturesque spot. The dogs love to stop there on both the trip down and back. Nellie approaches the hole delicately: keeping her paws out of the water, she takes a few small sips and is happy. Hector, on the other hand, trots to the waterhole, puts all his paws in and slurps it. And Muttley heads toward it at great speed, throws himself in bodily and gulps enthusiastically at the water. Then he stands perfectly still with a smile on his face and his eyes rolling back in his head: pure enjoyment, even as he starts sinking, unfazed, down into the mud. This happens every time and it always makes us laugh. When the other dogs start to move away, he quickly gathers his wits and races out dripping wet at such a pace that he doesn't realise his tail, heavy from the water, is his own, and begins to attack it. We all stand anticipating

Serendipitous beauty —

A mushroom sprouting after the rain,
a boat, a waterhole that vanishes in
high summer, a mysterious pair of
shoes perched on a rock – all shot
through with tones of lavender
and green. I always return from my
morning walks filled with ideas,
my head bursting with images.

his next move, which is invariably running toward one of us and shaking his wet fur in a frenzy.

We often meet one of the local farmers en route and they stop for a chat. If they have been collecting something from their land – fruit, vegetables, herbs or eggs – they generously share them with us. If it has been raining you sometimes encounter someone collecting snails. Living in a village surrounded by farmland has made me so much more conscious of what I eat; buying meat and fish in the city keeps you a step removed from its origins.

Walking back to the village provides the real exercise. The hills are steep and in summer the temperature slowly creeps up as the morning advances. Sometimes I just don't know how I manage it. The dogs show no signs of flagging and often run ahead, then wait ahead under the cool shade of a tree.

We drop Muttley off and nearly two hours after setting off Matthew, Hector, Nellie and I climb the last and steepest hill back to the village. We come in through the garden to the house, where our many cat friends wait, keenly anticipating their next meal. After feeding all the animals, Matthew and I settle down to a well-earned breakfast.

Ελιές
Olives

stratis

Vangelis

Around November, everyone rallies for the olive harvest. The olive trees (of which there are millions) are heavy with plump green and black fruit. Most are destined for local consumption.

A couple of village friends have invited me to join in when they start their harvest. The backbreaking work and the amount of acreage they cover over the many weeks of the harvest is astonishing. Fine weather makes the process much more palatable but there is always the risk of high winds and rain. Large nets are laid around the base of each tree, where families and friends work side-by-side, some hand-picking, others beating the trees with long thin sticks to shake out the olives.

The first harvest I attend is Gregory's. He grows seasonal produce throughout the year; his land, on the outskirts of the village, has breathtaking views to the sea and the weather conditions are perfect. Dandelions carpet the ground beneath the trees where Gregory and his over-excited golden retriever Pepe greet me. Nestled in the acres of fertile land with its many olive trees is a charming, simple one-roomed stone building where Gregory sometimes retreats from the summer village bustle. Pepe bounds over to welcome Nellie, but she's not keen on his attention and hides in the long grass. George, a young Albanian man who lives in the village, is Gregory's only helper, and with just the two of them, weeks of hard labour lie ahead.

As they handpick the olives and drop them into the nets, I am struck by their focus and tenacity. I help a little, picking out the debris before George scoops the olives into baskets and bags them for the press.

Shortly after I arrive, Gregory and George stop for something to eat. Lunch is simple: bread, a tin of beans warmed over a small portable gas cylinder, tinned fish and fresh tomatoes, with fruit to finish, all set up on a small table covered in a plastic floral cloth.

Pepe has been tied to a nearby tree as he's shamed himself by humping my leg. He looks on longingly, hoping for a tidbit or better yet, another chance to attach himself to my leg. Gregory builds a fire; he says it's for me. There is still warmth from the sun but the fire definitely adds a sense of occasion.

A week later Ralitza and I head off early in the morning to her land, in the opposite direction to Gregory's, away from the sea. The weather has changed and the temperature has dropped. A strong wind is blowing and the clear blue skies of the previous week have been replaced by thick grey clouds. We pass through a neighbouring village down a dirt road, wending our way through olive groves. I have not been here before; the rolling landscape is very different from Gregory's grove but just as beautiful, despite the weather.

We arrive in a valley thick with olive trees, all laden with fruit ripe for picking. I wander through the gate with Ralitza, who is keen to show me her olives and her land, which slopes down over rocks to end at a small flowing stream. The temperature is still high and as a result, there are an alarming number of mosquitoes. Add these to the hours of strenuous labour and the harvesting experience becomes excruciating. Ralitza has war wounds – multiple bites where the little bloodsuckers have bitten through her clothing the previous day. She is made from stronger stuff than I am; I am only able to help for a short while.

The picking team consists of Ralitza's son-in-law Stratis, his parents and Ralitza. Ralitza's daughter Mirisini has recently given birth to a son, Ignatis, so she does not come along. The nets are laid. Stratis and his father beat the trees with their long sticks and the women gather the olives that fall into the nets, putting them into loosely woven white feed bags which are secured at the top with a stick. At the end of each day, the bags are loaded into the back of Stratis's pick-up truck and driven to the local olive press just outside the village.

The press is run by Fotis, a jolly round man with a huge grey handlebar moustache. He holds the key to a machine room that houses the siren for the fire alert, which he has been known to sound at two in the morning. Whether this is down to over-consumption of ouzo or just plain mischievousness we will never know, but the sound is akin to a World War II air raid alert, extremely loud and very, very annoying. Thankfully this is an infrequent occurrence.

Fotis has two helpers at the olive press: Vangelis and Yiannis. Both work extremely hard, methodically pouring sacks of olives into a machine that resembles a Heath Robinson construction. Always keeping a keen eye on the machinery, they work fast as there is no time to lose. The more olives processed, the more money they make.

I cannot count the times that our generous friends have presented us with plastic bottles filled with their olive oil, so we were intrigued by the process for turning these luscious, plump fruits into smooth, golden olive oil. Each day huge sacks bursting with olives and labelled with the grower's name are dropped off at the press. Vangelis took great pride in showing us the workings of the operation and was keen for us to try some of the fresh oil, still warm from the press. He took a piece of bread from our local bakery, attached it to a stick and browned it in the burning furnace, then soaked it with the golden oil, topping it with a pinch of salt – so delicious!

We always appreciate our friends' gifts of both olives and oil, even more so now after the cherished time I have spent with both Gregory and Ralitza.

Ο κήπος της Ραλίτσας

Ralitza's garden

R alitza is a wonderful friend and neighbour. It is always a treat to sit with her in her hilltop garden and take in the stunning views. In summer, there is plenty of shade under a large walnut tree. We sit around a table and chat over a coffee or a cold drink, and she has usually prepared a sweet treat to share. Ralitza is such easy company with a marvellous sense of humour; she is patient and willing to explain Greek words and sentences to me.

Ralitza is always busy in her garden. In spring she plants vegetables and flowers; in summer she dries beans in the sun and sets aside fruit and vegetables for preserving. In autumn when the almonds fall, she hammers away at their shells, the noise reverberating into our garden. She also grows big marrows, preserves them in syrup and serves them as a welcoming sweet. Sometimes she sits separating and cleaning wool.

I passed Ralitza's garden one day to see that the gates were open and beyond them there was an open fire with an enormous old metal cauldron on top of it, bubbling away. The flames completely engulfed the bottom of the pot. I made my way up the path for a closer look. Ralitza explained that she was boiling figs from her tree to make syrup (*petimezi*), which she uses in cakes but also as an accompaniment for desserts. It is an essential ingredient in the honey cake made by another neighbour, Toula.

When I was a city dweller, there was a limited supply of fresh produce and I was only vaguely aware of seasonality. One of the greatest joys of island living is watching and helping my friends cultivate, pick, prepare, cook and preserve various foods. It is a meditative, communal and rewarding experience.

My neighbour Ralitza is constantly creative, whether
she is boiling figs for syrup or cleaning wool to spin.

Ralitza

Petimezi

I have given quantities to make 1 litre of syrup, but if you have your own tree, this recipe is a great way to make sure your figs don't go to waste, however many there are. You can also make a smaller quantity with fewer figs; simply adjust quantities to scale.

Place figs in a very large stockpot with enough water to cover them (approximately 10 litres). Bring to the boil over a high heat, then reduce the heat and simmer, covered, at medium heat for approximately 2 hours, stirring occasionally. Strain off the liquid, then boil it, uncovered, for a further 2 hours. Tie the herbs in muslin, add to the liquid and boil for another hour. Test the syrup by scooping some up with a ladle and letting it drip back into the pot. The syrup should be the consistency of honey; if it is still too thin, continue to boil until it reaches the desired thickness. Store in several small, clean jars.

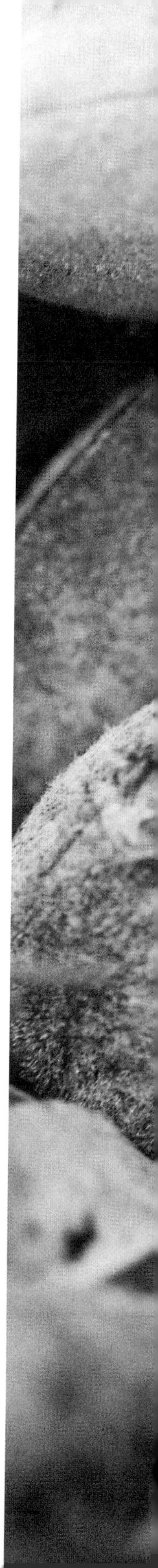

Makes 1 litre

4 kg fresh figs, rinsed well

water

3 stalks rosemary

3 stems basil

Η κουζίνα της Τούλας

Toula's kitchen

Everything from building a house
to making a cake is hands-on.

On one of our visits to George and Toula's house, we were treated to a delicious honey and walnut cake. It was unforgettable – Matthew is a particular fan – and, at his suggestion, I asked if I could put the recipe in this book.

George and Toula are always very generous to us. Over the years we have been given lots of delicious fruits and vegetables from their garden as well as home-baked cakes. Best of all was a present from George of honey, fresh from the hive. The honeycomb was attached to wire and presented in a handmade wooden frame. It looked so beautiful.

Toula speaks to me in a mixture of German and Greek; I don't always understand but with sign language we muddle through. Her son Vangelis occasionally translates for us, but the day these photos were taken, it was just the two of us in the kitchen. I watched carefully through the eye of my camera, asking questions along the way. The cake, her mother's recipe, is made often and lovingly. Toula instinctively throws the ingredients together, without any fuss.

All the ingredients are added to a large pink plastic bowl, one by one. Toula measures either by eye, or using one of two different-sized glasses – no-one uses scales, food processors or spatulas to make cakes here! A teaspoon and a tablespoon were also on hand for the cinnamon and flour. My favourite part came when Toula put both her strong hands into the mixing bowl and blended the ingredients together, repeating the kneading action many times.

She then scooped it all up and held her hand above the bowl, letting the heavy mixture drip slowly back into the bowl, repeating the process until she was happy with the consistency. She dropped it into the tin, which had been rubbed with her own olive oil, and scored the mixture with a knife several times before sprinkling it with sesame seeds.

The way Toula patted the mixture into the tin was sensual: she moved her hand around the top, clockwise and then anti-clockwise until it was ready for the oven. She told me to return in an hour to photograph the finished product.

When I returned she was distressed, as she had forgotten to turn the oven to the desired temperature for the final minutes and the cake was not quite ready. It was comforting for me, however, to discover that these things happen to the best and most experienced cooks and not just me.

When the cake was ready Toula cut it and insisted that I take half. She told me to share it with the friends I was meeting that afternoon. Once again I was touched by Greek generosity — this is typical of the way people share everything they have here.

Toula's honey and walnut cake

On Lesvos, nobody weighs ingredients – instead, large and small glasses are used to measure everything. Toula has made this cake so many times, she can tell by eye how much of each ingredient to use. I've given weights and measures here, but have also included the traditional glass measures in case you'd like to try them. If you don't want to make the petimezi, a jar of jam can be used instead.

Preheat the oven to 180° C and grease a 24 cm baking tin with olive oil.

Put all the dry ingredients except the sesame seeds into a large mixing bowl, make a well in the centre and add the eggs, syrup, water, honey and olive oil. Mix thoroughly by hand, over and over again, really getting everything to melt together. When the mixture has a smooth consistency, pour into the tin. Smooth the top with your hands, then use a fork to scrape around the edge of the tin, to prevent sticking.

Sprinkle with sesame seeds and then bake in the oven for 50–60 minutes, until golden brown. Allow to cool for 10 minutes before turning out.

Serves 12

1 large glass (250 ml) olive oil, plus extra for greasing
1 small glass (85 g) raisins
1 small glass (100 g) sugar
1 small glass (100 g) walnuts, chopped
1 teaspoon bicarbonate of soda
1 teaspoon salt
500 g self-raising flour
1 teaspoon cinnamon
2 eggs, beaten
1 large glass (250 ml) petimezi (see p 177 for recipe)
1 large glass (250 ml) water
1 small glass (300 g) honey
sesame seeds, for sprinkling

Φύση-Φροντίδα

Nature nurture

Nellie

I could not write this book without including the animals that have befriended us and the amazing people who devote their lives to helping them.

In the past, I had little time for animals. I lived in a pristine environment. I dressed in white, my floors and walls and furniture were white. I underwent a seismic shift when I came to the island and started my love affair with four-legged creatures. Now my friends laugh at the sight of me completely covered in all types of fur.

As I write this there are three cats inside the house. My special one, Sweetie, who is queen of the house; Mikraki, a small ginger cat, and Grey Bear, a cantankerous old tom with three legs. In the garden are Amanda, a sad-looking Big Balls, and Limpy. Nellie is asleep in her basket and Hector sits on the welcome mat. Outside the gate a handsome, high-spirited young male dog has just appeared, probably dumped by a passerby. Although there is no sign on our door saying 'Critters with any issues – abandonment to starvation – welcome', our home has become a refuge, and our days are filled with feeding, medicating, playing with and rescuing them.

We have become accustomed to the comings and goings of different cats through our garden. Our first visitor was a beautiful fluffy white-and-black female. She was shy and kept her distance until she trusted us enough to bring her kitten, a tiny ball of white fluff with piercing blue eyes. They visited for several months but never reappeared after one of our longer stays in London.

Lion Boy was next. He was named for his mane of golden fur, which became extremely thick in the winter to protect him from the harsh cold. He was cross-eyed and reminded us of Clarence from *Daktari*, a television program both Matthew and I had watched as children. A proud cat with a strong presence, he was always the first to arrive when we returned from London. Lion Boy would appear in the kitchen and let us know he wanted food. How he managed to get inside was a mystery to us; he seemed to have Houdini-like powers. He was clever; if he wasn't happy with what had been dished out, he would put his head behind the calico curtains where the food was kept and paw out another choice. He was not one to be made a fuss of and only occasionally, cautiously allowed us a pat. In the winter of 2008, Lion Boy came to say goodbye. He had developed skin cancer on his nose and a lump in his stomach. He stayed in the kitchen for a couple of nights, sleeping on a cosy rug by the radiator. One morning he went over to Matthew and wanted to be stroked. That was his way of saying goodbye; he was grateful for our companionship and we felt the same way. It was his time to go and he left us with dignity. We never saw our Lion Boy again. We still miss him hugely, as he was such a big part of our daily life.

Sweetie, a tri-coloured cat, was my special friend right from our first meeting. A bony, forlorn sight with gummy eyes, oily fur and loads of fleas, she jumped straight into my lap on a warm June evening when Domenica and I were sitting outside Ralitza's kafenio. She chose me over everyone else and our fate was sealed. Domenica and I knew that there was no way I could look after her because I was to-ing and fro-ing between London and Lesvos, but Ralitza came to the rescue. She volunteered to be the 'Aunty' and to make sure the kitten was looked after and fed whilst I was away. As Domenica and I climbed the hill home, the trusting kitten tucked, quivering, into the bend of my arm, I named her Sweetie.

The first few nights I kept her in my bedroom and cleaned her eyes, fed her and made her feel loved. After that I put a blanket in a box and placed it in the garden. I made the choice to put her outside early on, as I knew she needed to be independent and to integrate with the other cats. Ralitza fed her, but would never allow her in the house. Each morning at first light, I would hear Sweetie meowing; I'd go downstairs and see her dear little face and big green eyes peering over the top of the box. Over time she became healthy and fully enjoyed the life of a kitten. Even now she is still very much a kitten, always playing games, often presenting me with one of her toy mice as an offering. Ralitza is a good Aunty in my absence and looks after Sweetie very well. Ralitza says Sweetie guards her territory and always waits for my return.

One evening I heard a terrible noise in the garden. I could not work out what it was and went out to investigate. I cautiously approached the olive tree; curled up at its base was Foxy, a silver-grey and white male with horrific breathing difficulties. He sounded as if he should have been in intensive care. That wasn't his only problem; he was a neurotic mess, not knowing whether to purr or hiss. He always kept his distance, though over the years he did calm down a little. We were very fond of him and sad when in 2009 his respiratory system failed and he died.

The regular garden gang is made up of four other characters. Amanda is named after our friend Amanda. They share the same lovely, almond-shaped eyes that look as if they are outlined with kohl. Too late we realised that Amanda is male and so the name sticks. The origins of Big Balls and Squeaky's names are pretty self-explanatory. They are siblings; Big Balls is large and ginger-and-white, and Squeaky is small and affectionate with coarse fur in sludgy greys and rusts. Limpy is a white male with grey blotches – big, muscular and very affectionate. He often walks on three legs, hence the name. His limp doesn't hold him back; I have seen him lurching along the stone wall at the end of our garden on three legs in pursuit of a young female, and he sometimes walks through the village with Matthew and the dogs.

Key to our animal endeavours are Vasillia, Ineke and Joris. Vasillia first cared for our dog Nellie and has since become a friend. She has helped us with our many abandoned animals, and continues to love and board Nellie when we are away. Whenever we visit Vasillia, her many dogs bombard us, vying for our attention. Sometimes she has up to twenty-four animals of all shapes and sizes, rescued from all sorts of situations. Vasillia gives them security, love and food, and tries to find them homes, often sending them abroad.

We had often heard about Ineke and Joris, two wonderful people who run a wildlife rescue centre. They take in and give medical assistance to any injured, orphaned or sick animal. Another dedicated animal lover and rescuer gave us their number, for which we were recently extremely grateful. A very sad-looking fluffy male cat had wandered into our garden with his back leg a bleeding

stump and pain in his eyes. We took Grey Bear, as we named him, straight into the centre. Joris and two interns, dressed in the centre's uniform of head-to-toe army camouflage, met us at the entrance. They decided, very quickly, that it would be best to amputate what was left of Grey Bear's right hind leg. Given that he had been a feral cat, there were many ups and downs in his long, slow recovery; for one thing, he pulled out all his stitches immediately on waking from the anaesthetic.

After the operation, Ineke and Joris showed us around the hospital. We saw owls, sparrows, kestrels, eagles, honey buzzards, hawks, turtles, donkeys, snakes, and cats and dogs (all of which are either blind, partially sighted, deaf, or limbless). These rescued animals come not only from Lesvos but are also brought over from nearby islands. On arrival, every animal is logged in and its progress documented throughout its stay. Fully recovered animals are released back into the wild. One of the rehabilitated and released birds is a jackdaw who returns every day with offerings for the other birds, passing them into the cage.

Every morning Joris and Ineke rise at four-thirty to feed and medicate the animals. They clean all the cages and enclosures and do the paperwork relating to each one. It is a mammoth undertaking for two people. Sometimes, in summer, there are interns who come to observe and learn, but over the winter months Joris and Ineke are on their own with the help of an occasional volunteer – such as Matthew. He helps clean the aviaries once a week, assists with the occasional autopsy, and is learning how to administer medication. He really enjoys the work. We are completely awestruck by what Ineke and Joris have achieved. Without their love, care and medical experience, who knows what might have become of Grey Bear? Joris has renamed him Earl Grey.

My newest animal friend is a donkey whom I meet on my morning walks. When he sees me, he lets out an enormous bray, knowing that I have apples and carrots for him. I love the sound his chomping makes as it reverberates through his big box head. Whilst I caress Donkey's long, soft, furry ears, the dogs sniff around in the field. Muttley takes the end of the long rope Donkey is tethered to between his teeth and shakes his head from side to side, growling under his breath. This activity keeps him amused and stops him from bothering us. One morning I came around a bend in the road and found Donkey wandering free.

He let out the most enthusiastic bray yet and curled his lips, revealing a full set of teeth – an extra-special donkey smile. I felt so privileged. Then he came running towards me like a long-lost friend. I gave him an affectionate pat and tried to move on. Donkey wasn't having any of it. He picked up speed whenever I did, at times breaking into a trot. He wanted to be part of the crew, which I didn't mind. To my relief he stopped short of the village, as I didn't want anyone to think I had encouraged him or worse still, untied him. His owner is Stratis, the brother of Pandelis's wife Vasso. I couldn't find any of them, so I headed to Stratis's mother's. Her front room has become the village barbershop. Inside I could see Stratis giving someone a shave. It was an interesting challenge trying to explain my situation without knowing the Greek word for donkey. I was clutching at straws when I pulled out my phone and showed him the film of Donkey following me back to the village. Stratis was delighted. I cannot imagine what he thinks of me after that episode; I'm not even sure he understood why I was showing him. Perhaps he just sees an insane Australian walking through life with no end of animals following her. Not far from the truth.

There are so many more animal stories, some sad and some full of hope. Much needs to be done on Lesvos to raise awareness of animals. Educating the young is the first step. Programs for neutering need to be established and organisations like the EreSOS For Animals, run by our friend Gerbien, and the Lesbian Wildlife Hospital run by Joris and Ineke need donations and volunteers. Vasillia, Gerbien, Joris and Ineke are selfless individuals who do all that is humanly possible to improve the lives of these animals. Now it is up to the rest of us. Animals teach us so much, they deserve our respect and love.

Living on this beautiful island has been a blessing in so many ways. I have become connected not only to the animals but also to nature, the landscape and the community. My life here is full: the days pass quickly and my creativity is renewed. I enjoy simple pleasures: laughing with my friends, breathing the fresh air, flowing with the rhythm of the seasons and watching stars twinkle in the night sky. A journey that started as an occasional retreat from the big city has become a way of life. It all began with the love my parents gave me as a child, encouraging me to explore the world and enjoy life, and continues to this day with the affection I have found among the people of Lesvos.

Thank you
Thank you thank you...

Julie Gibbs
Eri Oetomo
Jocelyn Hungerford
Katrina O'Brien
and all at Penguin Lantern

Pippa Masson
Sharyn Storrier Lynham
Victoria Young
Francesca Hayles
Clem Gallagher
Domenica More Gordon
Ruth Brown
Amy Bullman
Elpida Stipsanou
Vasilia Mavrghani
Gerbine Fricke
Joris & Ineke Peeters-Lenglet
Ralitra, Mirsini & Stratis, Despina,
Toula, Irene, Gabriel and
his family, Konstantina and
her yiayia. Stratos, Panayiota,
Fotis, Pandelis and Vasso.

Matthew Usmar Lauder

The island of Lesvos
and all of our friends in the
village who have made
us so very welcome

Please don't forget the animals
who need our help
www.eresosforanimals.com

LANTERN

Published by the Penguin Group
Penguin Group (Australia)
250 Camberwell Road, Camberwell, Victoria 3124, Australia
(a division of Pearson Australia Group Pty Ltd)
Penguin Group (USA) Inc.
375 Hudson Street, New York, New York 10014, USA
Penguin Group (Canada)
90 Eglinton Avenue East, Suite 700, Toronto, Canada ON M4P 2Y3
(a division of Pearson Penguin Canada Inc.)
Penguin Books Ltd
80 Strand, London WC2R 0RL England
Penguin Ireland
25 St Stephen's Green, Dublin 2, Ireland
(a division of Penguin Books Ltd)
Penguin Books India Pvt Ltd
11 Community Centre, Panchsheel Park, New Delhi – 110 017, India
Penguin Group (NZ)
67 Apollo Drive, Rosedale, North Shore 0632, New Zealand
(a division of Pearson New Zealand Ltd)
Penguin Books (South Africa) (Pty) Ltd
24 Sturdee Avenue, Rosebank, Johannesburg 2196, South Africa

Penguin Books Ltd, Registered Offices: 80 Strand, London, WC2R 0RL, England

First published by Penguin Group (Australia), 2012

10 9 8 7 6 5 4 3 2 1

Cover design by Evi O © Penguin Group (Australia)
Text design by Evi O and Claire Lloyd © Penguin Group (Australia)
Photographs by Claire Lloyd
Endpapers: *Seascape* by Matthew Usmar Lauder
Typeset in Bodoni by Evi O
Colour reproduction by Splitting Image, Clayton, Victoria
Printed and bound in China by 1010 Printing International Ltd

National Library of Australia
Cataloguing-in-Publication data:

Lloyd, Claire
My Greek island home / Claire Lloyd.
9781921382581 (hbk.)
Lloyd, Claire.
Australians – Greece – Lesvos Island – Biography.
Lesvos Island (Greece) – Pictorial works.
Lesvos Island (Greece) – Description and travel.
Lesvos Island (Greece) – Social life and customs.

949.582

penguin.com.au/lantern